D1563625

LIMA

RYAN DUBÉ

Contents

Lima 5
Planning Your Time 7
History 7

Sights 11
Central Lima and Pueblo Libre 14
San Isidro and Miraflores 20
Barranco 23
Eastern Lima 25
Outside Lima 25

Entertainment
and Events 27
Nightlife 27
Cinemas 29
Performing Arts 30
Casinos 30
Spectator Sports 31
Festivals 31

Shopping 32
Handicrafts 32
Open-Air Market 33
Camping Equipment 33
Bookstores 34

Recreation 34
Cycling 34
Bird-Watching 34
Cooking 35
Horseback Riding 35

Paragliding 35
Scuba 35
Sea Kayaking 35
Surfing 35
Tour Agencies and Guides 36

Accommodations 37
Central Lima
and Pueblo Libre 37
San Isidro 38
Miraflores 40
Barranco 42

Food 43
Central Lima
and Pueblo Libre 43
San Isidro 45
Miraflores 46
Barranco and the South 50

Information
and Services 52
Visitor Information 52
Maps 52
Police and Fire 52
Immigrations Office 52
Health Care 52
Banks and Money Exchange 53
Communications 53
Newspapers 54
Language Schools 54

Film and Cameras................... 55

Laundry........................... 55

Luggage Storage 55

Getting There
and Around 55
Air................................ 55

Bus................................ 56

Train.............................. 57

Local Transportation................ 57

Southern Beaches 59
Punta Hermosa.................... 59

San Bartolo 61

LIMA

Lima's taxi drivers tend to be educated, perceptive, and opinionated. When asked what they think about Lima, they will tick off a litany of complaints: The highways are congested with buses. The air is full of exhaust and noise. Slums have sprawled across all the desert hills around Lima and residents there lack regular plumbing, water, and sometimes even electricity. The

HIGHLIGHTS

LOOK FOR  TO FIND RECOMMENDED SIGHTS, ACTIVITIES, DINING, AND LODGING.

C Catedral: After two decades of turbulence, Lima is roaring back, and at the center of it all is a refurbished main square and the 16th-century cathedral, with elegantly carved choir stalls and a huge painting gallery (page 14).

C Casa de Aliaga: This colonial mansion in the heart of Lima's old town is in pristine condition and offers a fascinating glimpse into domestic life during the opulent days of the viceroyalty (page 15).

C Museo de Sitio Bodega y Quadra: This museum, the former home of Spanish naval officer Juan Francisco de la Bodega y Quadra, is an example of the transition from colonial to republican life in Lima (page 16).

C San Francisco: This 16th-century convent has a brightly decorated patio and painting gallery upstairs, and labyrinthine catacombs downstairs (page 17).

C Museo Metropolitano de Lima: Travel through Lima's history via 3D movies and an earthquake simulator (page 18).

C Circuito Mágico del Agua: The biggest water fountain complex in the world has 13 interactive fountains and a light laser show (page 19).

C Museo Larco: With a huge collection of gold, textiles, and more than 40,000 ceramics, this museum offers a complete survey of all of Peru's archaeological treasures (page 20).

C Museo Nacional de Arqueología: The best way to wrap your mind around Peru's complex succession of ancient cultures is by visiting this compact and concise museum (page 20).

C Choco Museo: This unique museum offers chocolate lovers workshops on how to make chocolate while learning about the cacao tree (page 23).

C Bosque El Olivar: Stroll among more than 1,500 olive trees in this 450-year-old park (page 23).

© CARLOS SANTA MARIA/123RF

horse-drawn carriage in downtown Lima

an hour south of the city. And despite all its griminess, the center of Lima shines forth with a wealth of colonial art and architecture, rivaled perhaps only by Mexico City, the other great center of Spanish power in the New World.

The bottom line: Lima is an extraordinary city, but it takes a little getting used to. The country's leading museums, churches, and restaurants are here, along with nearly nine million people, almost one-third of Peru's population. It is the maximum expression of Peru's cultural diversity (and chaos). Whether you like it or not, you will come to Lima, because nearly all international flights land at this gateway.

PLANNING YOUR TIME

Depending on your interests, Lima can be seen in a day's dash or several days to take in most of the museums, churches, and surrounding sights. Peru travelers tend to enjoy Lima more at the end of a trip than at the beginning. After visiting Puno, Cusco, and other Peruvian cities, travelers are more prepared to deal with the logistics of getting around this huge city. They have also seen enough of the country to make better sense of the vast, and often poorly explained, collections in Peru's museums. Things start making sense.

If you are short on time and are visiting Cusco, one headache-free option is to fly from Cusco to Lima early in the morning and spend the day touring Lima on an organized tour (if you are planning on seeing Lima on your own, plan on one day for just acclimatizing). Various good day tours include lunch at one of the better restaurants in the city. You can head to the airport for your flight home in the evening, or early the following morning.

HISTORY

Present-day Lima was never the center of any great empire but rather a verdant valley where a series of cultures flourished alongside the shrine of **Pachacámac,** which by the Inca's time housed one of the most respected, and feared, oracles in the Andes. Huaca Pucllana, in Lima's upscale Miraflores neighborhood, was a ceremonial center built out of adobe bricks by

city's politicians and business leaders create a daily circus of corruption, and there is a huge, and growing, separation between the rich and the poor. Then, as if that weren't enough, there's the *garúa*. The blanket of fog rolls in from the ocean and covers everything May-November, depositing a patina of grime that lends the city its gray, dismal appearance.

But, in the same breath, the taxi driver will extol the virtues of this once-opulent capital of the Spanish viceroyalty that stretched from present-day Ecuador to Chile. Limeños are an exotic cocktail, a bit of coast, sierra, and rainforest blended with African, Chinese, and European to create an eclectic, never-before-seen blend. Heaps of tangy ceviche and succulent shellfish can be had for a few dollars, along with shredded chicken served in a creamy concoction of milk, mountain cheese, nuts, and *ají* pepper. Bars, clubs, and local music venues, called *peñas,* explode most nights with dance and the rhythms of *cumbia,* salsa, Afro-Peruvian pop, and a dozen forms of creole music. There are sandy beaches just half

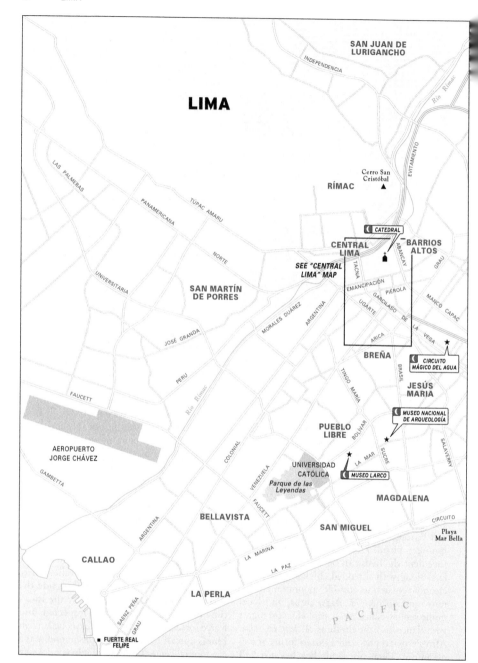

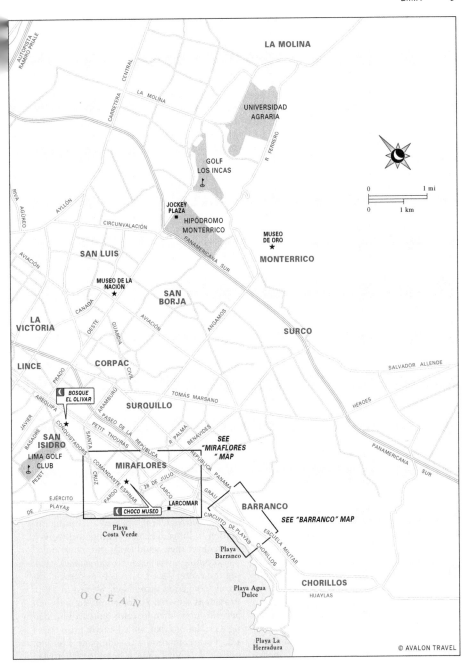

LA MOLINA

AUTOPISTA RAMIRO PRIALE

CENTRAL

CARRETERA

LA MOLINA

UNIVERSIDAD
AGRARIA

R FERRERO

GOLF
LOS INCAS

JOCKEY
PLAZA

HIPÓDROMO
MONTERRICO

PANAMERICANA SUR

MUSEO
DE ORO
★

MONTERRICO

RIVA
AGÜERO

AYLLÓN

CIRCUNVALACIÓN

AVIACIÓN

SAN LUIS

MUSEO DE LA
NACIÓN
★

SAN
BORJA

LA
VICTORIA

CANADA

OESTE

GUARDIA

AVIACIÓN

ANGAMOS

SURCO

SALVADOR ALLENDE

LINCE

PRADO

CORPAC

CIVIL

TOMÁS MARSANO

HEROES

ARAMBURU

AREQUIPA

(BOSQUE
EL OLIVAR

SURQUILLO

PANAMERICANA

JAVIER

BASADRE

CONQUISTADORES
★

PETIT THOURAS

PASEO DE LA REPÚBLICA

R PALMA

BENAVIDES

SUR

SAN
ISIDRO

SANTA

COMANDANTE ESPINAR

REPÚBLICA

SEE
"MIRAFLORES
" MAP

LIMA GOLF
CLUB

CRUZ

MIRAFLORES

2B DE JULIO

PANAMA

PEZET

PARDO ESPINAR

★

LARCO

GRAU

EJÉRCITO

DE

PLAYAS

(CHOCO MUSEO

LARCOMAR

BARRANCO

SEE "BARRANCO" MAP

CIRCUITO DE PLAYAS

ESCUELA MILITAR

Playa
Costa Verde

Playa
Barranco

CIRCUITO DE PLAYAS CHORILLOS

CHORILLOS

OCEAN

Playa Agua
Dulce

HUAYLAS

Playa La
Herradura

0   1 mi
0   1 km

© AVALON TRAVEL

the seafaring **Lima culture** from around AD 200 onward. The valley later fell under the influence of the Ayacucho-based **Huari culture** and was integrated by 1300 into the **Ychma kingdom,** which built most of the monumental architecture at Pachacámac. The Inca **Túpac Yupanqui** conquered the area in the mid-15th century and built an enclosure for holy women alongside Pachacámac's stepped pyramid.

The first Spaniard to arrive in the area was **Hernando Pizarro,** who rode with a group of soldiers from Cajamarca in 1533 to investigate reports of gold at Pachacámac. They found nothing, but his brother, Francisco, returned two years later to move the capital here from Cusco. **Francisco Pizarro** was drawn to the spot because of its fertile plains and the natural port of Callao. (Both Pizarros had come here in January, in the middle of Lima's brief summer, and must have thought it was a sunny place.)

Pizarro laid the city out in typical checkerboard pattern, with the main square butting up against the **Río Rímac** ("talking river" in Quechua), a natural defensive line. He christened Lima **Ciudad de Los Reyes** (City of the Kings), and a decade later it was designated the capital of the Spanish viceroyalty in South America and eventually seat of the continent's archbishop. **Universidad San Marcos,** America's first university, was founded here in 1511, and the city was completely walled by the 17th century.

Most of the Roman Catholic orders established themselves in Lima and built more than a dozen baroque churches and convents. Even the Spanish Inquisition for South America was based here (its headquarters is now an interesting museum). By royal decree, all the commerce of the entire viceroyalty—essentially the entire west side of South America—had to pass through Lima, fueling a construction boom of elegant homes and promenades, such as the Paseo de Aguas on the far side of the Río Rímac (these days a downtrodden neighborhood).

The city was quickly rebuilt after a devastating 1746 earthquake that destroyed 80 percent of its structures and slammed the port of **Callao** with a 12-meter tsunami. Lima's prominence began to fade after the independence wars of the 1820s, when it lost its monopoly over South American commerce.

Even in the early days of Lima, neighborhoods of black, indigenous, and mixed-race workers began to crop up around the city, and the expansion continued after the city's walls were torn down by **President José Balta** (in office 1868-1872). During the **War of the Pacific** (1879-1883), Lima was sacked by an invading Chilean army, which carted off church gold and most of the national library's books to Santiago de Chile.

There had always been a main avenue leading through the countryside to the port of Callao, but as the city expanded, other principal avenues were built outside the center, and the city's first electric train was inaugurated in 1906. For four centuries Lima had been a small city, and even in 1919 only had 173,000 inhabitants. Over the rest of the 20th century, Lima's population would swell to its current size of nearly nine million.

As in other South American capitals, Lima's population exploded as the country transitioned from a rural economy to one based on large industry. Impoverished campesinos migrated here from the countryside and built ramshackle slums, called *pueblos jóvenes*. Since the mid-1990s, these slums have turned into full-fledged neighborhoods, some of which are now working class, with Internet access and big grocery stores. Others are still very poor, lacking running water and sewer services.

Lima's poverty became intense during the 1980s and 1990s, when a series of countryside massacres committed by both the **Shining Path** and the Peruvian army sparked a crushing migration to Lima. The new immigrants worked at whatever they could find, and many ended up becoming street vendors (*ambulantes*), causing the center's main streets to become completely congested. After being elected in 1990, **President Alberto Fujimori** put an end—albeit through corrupt techniques and human rights violations that landed him in prison with a 25-year sentence—to the rampant inflation, rolling blackouts, and car bombings that were terrorizing Lima residents. In 1992, he captured **Abimael Guzmán,** the former philosophy professor who founded and led the Shining Path. **Túpac Amaru,** the country's other main guerilla group, staged a final stand in Lima in 1996 by taking 490 hostages during a gala at the Japanese ambassador's residence. The standoff ended four months later after a Peruvian special forces team freed the hostages, killing the 14 guerillas in the process (only one hostage died—of bleeding from a gunshot wound).

Even before the terrorism years, much of the commerce and most of the wealthy families had abandoned the center of Lima and established the upscale neighborhoods and corporate centers of Monterrico, Miraflores, and San Isidro, where nearly all of the city's best hotels and restaurants are now located.

Though still a bit grimy and unsafe to walk around in at night, the center of Lima is making a comeback. Street vendors were banned in the mid-1990s, and now the Plaza de Armas has been renovated with new riverside promenades and a spate of nice restaurants. Businesses like *Caretas,* the country's leading newsmagazine, have moved back to the center. Compared to the mid-1990s, the center of Lima feels pleasant and safe.

Sights

Lima can be thought of as a triangle, with the city center at the apex. The base begins with the port of **Callao** and the nearby airport and runs along the coast through the neighborhoods of **Miraflores, Barranco,** and **Chorillos.** Other

Plaza Mayor at night

© HOLGS/ISTOCKPHOTO.COM

neighborhoods, such as **Pueblo Libre** and **San Isidro,** are in the middle of the triangle.

Lima is jam-packed with sights, but most interesting to many people are the colonial churches, convents, and homes in Lima's center, which is safe but warrants precautions nonetheless: Leave your passport and money in the hotel, and guard your camera. Also keep an eye on your bag when at a restaurant.

Lima's best museums are spread out, set in neighborhoods that are sandwiched between the coast and the center. Excellent collections of pre-Columbian gold, textiles, and ceramics can be found at the Museo Larco in Pueblo Libre, Museo de la Nación in San Borja, and Museo de Oro in Monterrico. English-speaking and sometimes French-speaking guides are usually available at these museums.

Most Lima visitors stay in San Isidro, Miraflores, and Barranco, neighborhoods near the coast with the best selection of hotels, restaurants, and nightlife. There is little to see here, however, except for giant adobe platforms that were built by the Lima culture (AD 200-700) and now rise above the upscale neighborhoods.

There are so many sights to see in downtown Lima that you would need a few days to see them all. The best idea is to start early

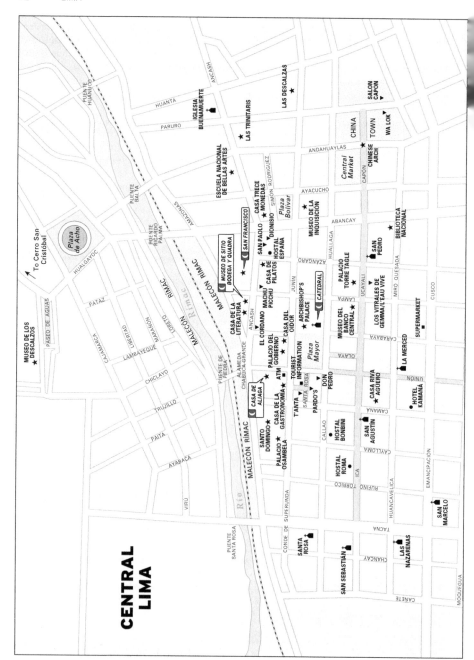

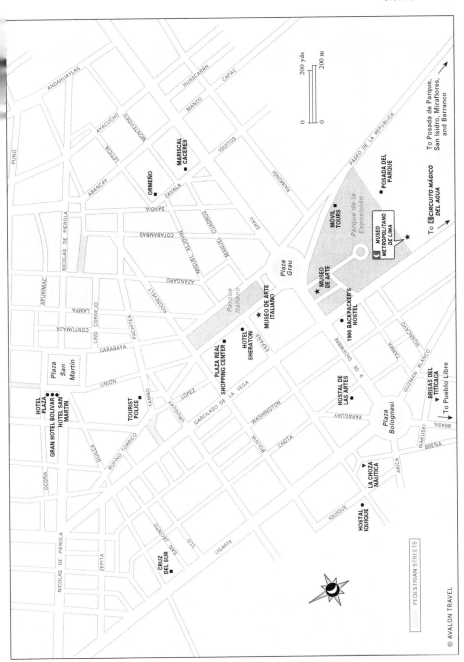

200 yds

200 m

To Posada de Parque,
San Isidro, Miraflores,
and Barranco

MARISCAL CÁCERES ■

ORMEÑO ●

POSADA DEL PARQUE ●

MOVIL TOURS ■

Parque de la Exposición

MUSEO METROPOLITANO DE LIMA ℹ

To ⊞ CIRCUITO MÁGICO DEL AGUA

Plaza Grau

MUSEO DE ARTE ★

1900 BACKPACKER'S HOSTEL ●

Parque Italiano

MUSEO DE ARTE ITALIANO ★

HOTEL SHERATON ●

PLAZA REAL SHOPPING CENTER ■

HOSTAL DE LAS ARTES ●

Plaza San Martín

HOTEL PLAZA ●
GRAN HOTEL BOLIVAR ●
HOTEL SAN MARTÍN ●

TOURIST POLICE ■

Plaza Bolognesi

BRISAS DEL TITICACA ▼

To Pueblo Libre

LA CHOZA NÁUTICA ▼

HOSTAL IQUIQUE ●

CRUZ DEL SUR ■

PEDESTRIAN STREETS

© AVALON TRAVEL

© CARLOS SALA/PROMPERU

Lima's Catedral on the Plaza Mayor

with the big sights, be selective, and work your way down the list as energy allows. The old town is bordered by the Río Rímac to the north, Avenida Tacna to the west, and Avenida Abancay to the east. The center of Lima is perfectly safe, but it is a good idea not to stray too far outside these main streets—except for a lunchtime foray to Chinatown or a taxi ride to Museo de los Descalzos, on the other side of the river. Mornings are best reserved for visits to Lima's main churches, which are mostly open 8am-1pm and 5pm-8pm daily and have English-speaking guides who request a tip only. Taxis into the center from Miraflores cost US$5 (15-30 minutes). For public transportation, there are a couple of options, with the best choice being the **Metropolitano,** the new rapid bus system. Its buses run straight from Barranco through Miraflores and to the downtown center and back. There are several stations in Miraflores located on the Vía Expresa (15-20 minutes, www.metropolitano. com.pe, US$1). The other option is to head to Arequipa Avenue and catch a *Todo Arequipa*

bus that runs within walking distance of the center (30-50 minutes, US$0.50). Arequipa Avenue is one of the main streets in Lima connecting the center to Miraflores. These buses run the entire avenue.

CENTRAL LIMA AND PUEBLO LIBRE
◖ Catedral

Start on the **Plaza Mayor,** which is graced with a bronze fountain from 1650 and flanked on one side by the **Catedral,** which was built in the late 16th century. It contains the carved wooden sepulcher of Francisco Pizarro, who was murdered in 1541 by a mob of Almagristas, a rival political faction. As you enter, the first chapel on the right is dedicated to St. John the Baptist and contains a carving of Jesus that is considered to be among the most beautiful in the Americas. But the highlights of the cathedral are the choir stalls carved in the early 17th century by Pedro Noguera and the **museum** (9am-5pm Mon.-Fri., 10am-1pm Sat., 1pm-5pm Sun., US$3.50). Paintings here include a

1724 work by Alonso de la Cueva that portrays the faces of the 13 Inca rulers alongside a lineup of Spanish kings from Carlos V to Felipe V. There is no clearer example of how art was used to put order on a turbulent, violent succession of kings. Other pieces include a series of allegorical paintings created in the 17th century by the Bassano brothers in northern Italy (no one knows how or when this priceless art was imported) and chest altars, one from Ayacucho and the other from Cusco, with an astounding number of miniature painted figures made of potato flour.

Also on the Plaza Mayor are the magnificent **Archbishop's Palace,** which mainly has religious art, and, on the corner, the **Casa del Oidor.** This 16th-century house has Lima's signature wooden balconies on the outside, with carvings inspired by Moorish designs and wood slats from behind which women viewed the activity on the square. Next door is the **Palacio del Gobierno,** the president's palace, which forms the other side of the Plaza Mayor and was built by the Spanish on top of the home of Taulichusco, the ruler of the Rímac Valley at that time. It was at this spot that liberator José de San Martín proclaimed the symbolic independence of Peru on July 28, 1821. There is an interesting change of the guard (noon Mon.-Sat.) and a change of the flag (5:45pm Mon.-Sat.).

Also on the Plaza Mayor is the **Municipality of Lima** and the **Club de la Unión,** a business club formed in 1868 that is a bit empty these days. Between these buildings are the pedestrian streets of Pasaje Santa Rosa and Escribanos, which are lined with upscale restaurants, cafés, and bookstores. At the corner of the palace and the Municipality is where Lima's antique post office, the **Casa de Correos y Telégrafos,** used to be located. It has now been turned into **La Casa de la Gastronomía Peruana,** a museum celebrating Peruvian cuisine (176 Conde de Superunda, tel. 01/426-7264, 9am-5pm Tues.-Sun., US$1). Behind the museum is the pedestrian walkway **Pasaje de Correos,** which had a glass roof until a 1940 earthquake destroyed it and is now lined with vendors selling postcards, teddy bears, and other miscellaneous items.

◖ Casa de Aliaga

A half-block from the Plaza Mayor down Unión is **Casa de Aliaga** (Unión 224, tel. 01/427-7736, www.casadealiaga.com, 9am-5pm daily, US$10), which was built in 1535 and is the oldest home on the continent still family-owned, after 17 generations. It is one of the best-preserved colonial homes in Peru, with a series of salons representing decor from the 16th, 17th, and 18th centuries. The land for the home was first deeded to Jerónimo de Aliaga, one of the 13 men who remained with Francisco Pizarro during his grueling exploration of Peru's coast in 1527. You can visit on your own, but in-house guides speak Spanish only. For English-speaking tours, try **Lima Tours** (tel. 01/619-6900).

Santo Domingo and Lima Riverfront

Near the Plaza Mayor is **Santo Domingo,** on the corner of Camaná and Conde de Superunda. This church was built in 1537 by the Dominicans and was remodeled in neoclassic style in the 19th century. At the end of the right nave is the Retablo de las Reliquias (Altar of the Relics), with the skulls of the three Peruvian Dominicans to reach sainthood. From left to right, they are San Martín de Porras, Santa Rosa, and San Juan Macias. Next door is the attached **convent** (8:30am-5:30pm daily, US$2.50), with carved balconies around a patio, fountains covered with Seville tiles, and a library with colossal 17th-century choir books. This convent was the first location of the Americas' first university, **San Marcos,** and the balcony where students read their theses can still be seen in the Sala Capitular. The convent is open until 5:30pm, but get there by 4:30pm if you want to catch the last tour.

Also on the street Conde de Superunda is **Palacio Osamblea** (Superunda 298, 9:30am-5pm Mon.-Fri., free), a neoclassic rose-colored home with five elegant balconies. It has been converted into a space for rotating exhibitions

Colonial Vs. Republican Homes

The differences between colonial (1534-1822) and republican (1820-1900) homes are clear in theory but muddled in practice. Most of Peru's old homes were built in colonial times by Spaniards who received prized plots on or near the Plaza de Armas. These houses, passed down from generation to generation, were often restored in the 19th or early 20th century with republican elements. So most houses, or *casonas*, are somewhat of a blend. But all share in common the basic Spanish layout: a tunnel-like entry, or *zaguán*, leads into a central courtyard, or *traspatio*. The rooms are built with high ceilings and a second-story wood balcony around the courtyard. The homes of the wealthy have stone columns, instead of wood, and additional patios.

During the nearly three centuries of the Peruvian viceroyalty, homes went from the solid fortified construction of medieval times to the more intricate decorations of the baroque, which were often based on Mudejar, or Arabic, patterns brought from Spain. After independence, however, homes demonstrate neoclassic elegance and the more confident use of colors favored in the New World, such as bright blues, greens, and yellows.

COLONIAL HOMES

- *Traspatios* paved with *canto rodado* (river stones)
- Sparse interiors
- Heavy brown and green colors
- Simple ceilings, often made of plaster, cane, and tile
- Baroque or rococo decorations with Mudejar patterns
- Forged iron windows with intricate lace patterns
- *Celosia* balconies where women could observe but not be observed

REPUBLICAN HOMES

- *Traspatios* paved with polished stone slabs
- Elegant interior decorations and furniture
- Light yellow, white, and blue colors
- Elaborate, often carved, wooden ceilings
- Neoclassic decorations with ornate columns

hosted by the Centro Cultural Garcilaso de la Vega. Ask the doorman for a tour (in Spanish). Tips are appreciated.

Alameda Chabuca Grande is a new riverfront public space, within a block of the Plaza Mayor, that is dedicated to one of Peru's best-known musicians, whose creole music is famous worldwide. The space, used by musicians and artists, is generally safe to walk around until 9pm, when the security guards go home.

The Río Rímac, brown with mud and clogged with plastic, tumbles by. Across the river, the Rímac neighborhood was populated by mestizos and other people of mixed race during colonial times. The large hill on the other side is **Cerro San Cristóbal.** Walk upriver along Ancash to Desamparados, Lima's beautiful old train station that has been

converted into the **Casa de la Literatura Peruana** (Ancash 207, tel. 01/426-2573, www.casadelaliteratura.gob.pe, 10:30am-8pm Tues.-Sun., free) a library dedicated to Peruvian authors like Mario Vargas Llosa, José María Arguedas, and Cesar Vallejo.

◖ Museo de Sitio Bodega y Quadra

Just down the street is the new **Museo de Sitio Bodega y Quadra** (Ancash 213, tel. 01/738-2163 or 01/428-1644, 9am-5pm Tues.-Sun.), which shows the transition of colonial and republican life in Lima. The city has spent the last several years excavating and restoring the lower portion of the house, which highlights colonial-era floors and structures. The 18th-century house was the home of Juan Francisco

© CARLOS IBARRA/PROMPERU

the facade of the San Francisco church

de la Bodega y Quadra, a Spanish naval officer who explored Canada's Pacific coast.

(San Francisco

San Francisco (Ancash and Lampa, 9:30am-5:30pm daily, US$2.50, US$1.50 students) is a 16th-century convent featuring a patio lined with centuries-old *azulejos* (Seville tiles) and roofed with *machimbrado,* perfectly fitted puzzle pieces of Nicaraguan mahogany. There are frescoes from the life of Saint Francis of Assisi, a 1656 painting of the Last Supper with the disciples eating guinea pig and drinking from gold Inca cups (*qeros*), and a series of paintings from Peter Paul Rubens's workshop depicting the passion of Christ. But the highlight is the catacombs, or public cemetery, where slaves, servants, and others without money were buried until 1821 (rich citizens were usually buried in their home chapels). The underground labyrinth is a series of wells, some 20 meters deep, where bodies were stacked and covered with lime to reduce odor and disease. After they

decomposed, the bones were stacked elsewhere. Across the street from San Francisco is **Casa de Pilatos** (Ancash 390, closed to the public), a colonial home that is occupied by Peru's Constitutional Tribunal.

Museo de la Inquisición

Casa de las Trece Monedas (Ancash 536, closed to the public) was built in 1787 and gets its name from the 13 coins in the coat of arms on its facade. Nearby is **Plaza Bolívar,** flanked by Peru's congress building and graced with a bronze statue in honor of liberator Simón Bolívar. On the far side of the plaza is the interesting **Museo de la Inquisición** (www.congreso.gob.pe/museo.htm, 9am-5pm daily, free), which served as the headquarters of the Spanish Inquisition from 1570 until it was abolished in 1820. The museum explains the harsh and bizarre punishments that the church doled out for crimes that included heresy, blasphemy, seduction, and reading banned books. There are creepy dungeon-like spaces in the back where the punished were given 50 lashes and jailed while others were sent to work on slave ships or in public hospitals. This was also where autos-da-fé were ordered—public condemnation ceremonies in the Plaza de Armas where witches, bigamists, and heretics were hanged to death or burned at the stake.

Chinatown

Chinatown is an excellent place to have lunch or late-afternoon tea, in the midst of a neighborhood founded by Chinese indentured workers, called coolies, who came here after finishing their contract on the train lines or coastal haciendas. The main street is **Capón,** which has three **Asian temples,** a **Chinese arch,** and a variety of stores and restaurants. The entire Chinatown area is adjacent to Lima's **central market.**

Historic Downtown

The 16th-century **San Pedro** (Azángaro and Ucayali, hours vary, free) has a drab mannerist facade but has one of the most spectacular church interiors in Peru. Huge white arching ceilings lead to a magnificent altar covered in gold leaf and designed by Matías Maestro, who is credited for bringing the neoclassic style to Peru. At the end of the right nave, ask permission to see the mind-blowing sacristy, decorated with tiles and graced with a magnificent painting of the coronation of the Virgin Mary by Peru's most famous painter, Bernardo Bitti. Painted on the ceiling boards above are scenes from the life of San Ignacio. If you come in the morning, it is possible to ask permission to see the cloisters and two interior chapels as well.

Palacio Torre Tagle (Ucayali 363) is a mansion built in 1735 that is, like Casa de Aliaga, in pristine condition. Visits can be arranged by popping into the Ministry of Foreign Affairs next door at Ucayali 318. At the **Museo del Banco Central** (tel. 01/613-2000, 10am-4:30pm Mon.-Fri.,10am-1pm Sat.-Sun., free), the ground floor holds a colonial money exhibit, one flight up is a 19th- and 20th-century painting gallery, and the basement shines with pre-Columbian ceramics and textiles (including a range of intriguing Chanca pieces). The paintings include a good selection of watercolors from Pancho Fierro (1807-1879), paintings from 20th-century artist Enrique Polanco, and etchings by Cajamarca's indigenous artist José Sabogal (1888-1956).

The church of **San Agustín** (Ica and Camaná, hours vary, free) has an 18th-century baroque facade that is one of the most intricate in the Americas and looks almost as if it were carved from wood, not stone. **Casa Riva Agüero** (Camaná 459, tel. 01/626-6600, 10am-1pm and 2pm-5pm Mon.-Fri., US$7, US$1.75 museum only), an 18th-century home with all original furniture, has an interesting museum of colonial handicrafts as well as ceramics and textiles from the Lima culture.

Other interesting churches, which are clustered together, are **La Merced** (Unión and Miró Quesada, hours vary, free), which was built in 1754 and holds a baroque *retablo* carved by San Pedro de Nolasco; and **San Marcelo** (Rufino Torrico and Emancipación, hours vary, free). Nearby are three 17th-century churches within four blocks of each other on the busy Avenida Tacna: **Las Nazarenas** (6am-noon and 5pm-8:30pm daily, free), which holds the image of El Señor de los Milagros, the city's patron saint, whose October festival draws as many as a half million celebrants; **San Sebastián** (hours vary, free); and **Santa Rosa** (9:30am-noon and 3:30pm-7pm daily, free).

Art Museums

If you are taking a taxi from San Isidro or Miraflores into the center, you will travel along a sunken highway known as the **Vía Expresa** (also nicknamed "El Zanjón," or The Ditch). The highway emerges on ground level and passes along a series of public parks before entering old town. One of these is the **Parque de la Exposición,** which was built in the 19th century and is still thriving today. The park is ringed with a high fence and is best entered at the corner of 28 de Julio and Garcilaso de la Vega. The park has an artificial lake full of goldfish, gardens with lounging turkeys, and the **Kusi Kusi Puppet Theater** (basement of the German-style gingerbread house, tel. 01/477-4249, US$4, US$2.50 children), which has Sunday performances. Here too is the **Museo de Arte** (Paseo Colón 125, Parque de la Exposición, tel. 01/204-0000, www.mali.pe, 10am-8pm Tues.-Fri., 10am-5pm Sat., 10am-8pm Sun., US$4 adults, US$1.50 students), which houses the best range of Peruvian paintings in the country, an espresso bar, and a cinema. The museum contains colonial furniture, some pre-Columbian ceramics, and a huge collection of paintings from the viceroyalty to the present. Another nearby park is the **Parque Italiano,** which contains the **Museo de Arte Italiano** (Paseo de la República 250, tel. 01/423-9932, 10am-5pm Mon.-Fri., US$3), with a collection of European art mainly from the early 20th century.

◖ Museo Metropolitano de Lima

Also located in the Parque de la Exposición is the new **Museo Metropolitano de Lima** (tel. 01/433-7122, 9:30am-5pm Tues.-Sun., US$2), which provides a virtual tour of Lima's history,

the Museo de Arte in Lima's Parque de la Exposición

complete with 3-D movies and an earthquake simulator. After seeing several museums and churches, this is a good way to bring all that history together. If you don't speak Spanish, it is best to bring a translator.

🄲 Circuito Mágico del Agua

The **Circuito Mágico del Agua** (Petit Thouars Esquina with Jr. Madre de Dios, tel. 01/330-3052, www.parquedelareserva.com.pe, 3pm-10:30pm Wed.-Sun., US$2, free under age 5) is a popular attraction for locals. It has 13 interactive fountains and a light and laser show. The place is said to be the biggest fountain complex in the world. The fountains are within the 8-hectare **Parque de la Reserva,** which was built in 1929 to honor reservists that defended Lima from Chilean armies during the 19th century War of the Pacific. The park was recently restored after years of neglect and is now in pretty good shape. Among its gardens you'll find Italian-inspired archways and a statue to honor independence fighter Antonio José de Sucre. The yellow house in the middle of the park was designed by José Sabogal, the father of Peru's indigenist art movement.

Rímac

Right across the Río Rímac from Lima is the downtrodden Rímac neighborhood, which began as a mixed-race barrio during the viceroyalty and was refurbished in the 18th century by the Lima aristocracy. All the sights here are close to the Plaza de Armas—take a taxi, as assaults are common in this area.

The **Museo de los Descalzos** (end of Alameda Los Descalzos, tel. 01/481-0441, 9:30am-1pm and 2pm-5:30pm daily, $2) was a convent and spiritual retreat for the Franciscans. Today it contains interesting and elegant cloisters, a chapel with a gold-covered baroque altar, an elegant refectory, and a gallery with more than 300 paintings from the 17th and 18th centuries—including a masterpiece by Esteban de Murillo. On the taxi ride home, ask your driver to pass the nearby **Paseo de Aguas,** an 18th-century French-style promenade where Lima's elites strolled along its artificial waterways. All that remains today is a neoclassic arch, hidden next to a towering Cristal Beer factory. Nearby is the giant **Plaza de Acho,** Lima's bullring, where **bullfights** (early Oct.-early Dec.) are held. Inside is the **Museo Taurino** (Hualgayoc 332, tel. 01/481-1467, 9am-6pm Mon.-Sat., US$2.50), which contains a wide range of bullfighting relics.

Towering above Rímac is **Cerro San Cristóbal,** where Francisco Pizarro placed a cross in thanks that Quizo Yupanqui and his Inca army did not succeed in crossing the Río Rímac into Lima during the Inca rebellion of 1536. Today the hill is encrusted with a dusty *pueblo jóven* named Barrios Altos. There is a lookout over Lima at the top, along with a small museum and a giant cross that is illuminated at night. To reach the top, take a taxi from the Plaza de Armas (US$6 one-way). Ask the taxi to wait for you at the top to bring you back to the Plaza de Armas. The area is rough and reports of muggings are common, so don't try walking back to the plaza.

◖ Museo Larco

The charming neighborhood of **Pueblo Libre** is just south of central Lima and has a more relaxed, small-town vibe. Its best-known sight is the **Museo Larco** (Bolívar 1515, tel. 01/461-1312, www.museolarco.org, 9am-10pm daily, US$11), which rivals the Museo de Oro in terms of gold pieces and has far more ceramics and textiles. Founded in 1926 in an 18th-century mansion built atop a pre-Hispanic ruin, this museum has more than 40,000 ceramics and 5,000 pieces of gold and textiles. There are huge Mochica earrings and funerary masks, a Paracas textile with a world-record 398 threads per inch, and a jewelry vault filled with gold and silver objects. A back storage room holds thousands of pre-Hispanic ceramic vessels, including a Moche erotic collection that will cause even the most liberated to blush. There is an excellent on-site restaurant, and it is easy to reach by bus from Miraflores. Catch a bus at Arequipa Avenue that says "Todo Bolívar" and get off at the 15th block.

◖ Museo Nacional de Arqueología

A 15-minute walk away from Museo Larco is Pueblo Libre's laid-back Plaza Bolívar and the **Museo Nacional de Arqueología, Antropología, e Historia** (Plaza Bolívar s/n, Pueblo Libre, tel. 01/463-5070, http://museonacional.perucultural.org.pe, 9:30am-5pm Tues.-Sat., US$5 includes tour). Although smaller than the Museo de la Nación, this museum presents a clearer, certainly more condensed, view of Peruvian history, and linked with the Museo Larco, it makes for a complete day in central Lima. Exhibits include Moche ceramics, Paracas tapestries, Chimú gold, and scale models for understanding the hard-to-see Chavín and Huari sites.

The museum's most important piece is the Estela Raimondi, a giant stone obelisk that once graced one of Peru's first ceremonial centers, Chavín de Huantár (1300-200 BC), near present-day Huaraz. It is carved with snakes, pumas, and the first appearance of the Dios de los Báculos (Staff-Bearing God), which would reappear, in different incarnations, throughout Peru's ancient history. The tour includes a walk through the adjacent colonial home where independence leaders José de San Martín and Simón Bolívar stayed.

Around the corner is the 16th-century **Iglesia Magdalena** (San Martín and Vivanco), which has attractive carved altars and a gold painting of Señor de los Tremblores (Lord of the Earthquakes). An excellent restaurant, café, and pisco-tasting bodega, all steeped in tradition, are down the street.

SAN ISIDRO AND MIRAFLORES

What appears to be a clay hill plunked down in the middle of Miraflores is actually a huge adobe pyramid from the Lima culture, which built a dozen major structures in and around what is now Lima AD 200-700. **Huaca Pucllana** (General Bolognesi 800, Miraflores, tel. 01/617-7148, www.huacapucllanamiraflores.pe, 9am-5pm Wed.-Mon., US$4) has a small but excellent museum that includes ceramics, textiles, reconstructed tombs, and artifacts from this culture that depended almost entirely on the sea for survival. A recently discovered pot shows a man carrying a shark on his back—proof that this culture somehow hunted 450-kilogram sharks. No free wandering is allowed, but guides lead tours every 30 minutes around the ceremonial plazas and a few inner rooms. This is a good option for those who cannot see the larger Pachacámac, 31 kilometers south of Lima. There is an upscale and delicious restaurant on-site that serves Peruvian cuisine with a modern twist.

A similar, though completely restored, stepped pyramid in San Isidro is **Huaca Huallamarca** (Nicólas de Piérola 201, tel. 01/222-4124, 9am-5pm Tues.-Sun., US$3.50), which offers a chance to understand what these temples once looked like. From the top, there is an interesting view over Lima's most upscale district.

Museo de Historia Natural (one block west of the 12th block of Arequipa, Arenales

SAN ISIDRO

To Central Lima

BURGOS
BARCELONA
LA BONBONNIERE

AV. SALAVERRY
ROMA
CASTAÑOS
MORERAS
PORRES OSORES
LOS EUCALIPTOS
LAS FLORES
LAS LAURELES
LOS NOGALES
LOS CEDROS
LOS ROSALES
LOS ALAMOS
DOS DE MAYO
LOS NARANJOS
CIPRESES
FICUS
JAVIER PRADO OESTE
LOS PALMERAS
LOS SAUCES
LOS PINOS
LOS FRESNOS
LOS OLIVOS
AV. ARENALES
JAVIER PRADO ESTE

ELESPURI
SAN ISIDRO GOLF
JOSÉ GRANDA
LOS DELFINES
COUNTRY CLUB LIMA HOTEL/
EL PERROQUET
ORRANTIA
NICOLAS DE RIVERA

To Cafeladeria 4D
and José
Antonio

LOFT
MANUEL
BAÑON
AREQUIPA
YOUTH HOSTAL
MALKA
LOS LIRIOS
Parque de
las Americas
LAS CAMELIAS

MALABAR
SANTA LUISA
BELAUNDE
SWISSÓTEL
SANTA TRADICIONES
TANTA
COMO AGUA
PARA CHOCOLATE
TORIBIO
PAZ SOLDAN
SONESTA EL OLIVAR
TAMAYO
24 DE ABRIL

CHOQUEHUANCA
ANDES
AURELIO MIRO QUESADA
ALZAMORA
REAL

LIMA GOLF CLUB

ICE CREAM FACTORY
CAMINO
E PLÁSCENIA
SEGUNDO MUELLE
PANCHO FIERRO
LA LINTERNA
CAVERO
Parque
El Olivar
PETIT THOURAS

JUAN ANTONIO PESET
CERVANTES
CLEMENT
EGUIGUREN
CONDE DE LA
MONCLOVA
ALVAREZ CALDERON
ROAUD
LIBERTADORES
DON MAMINO
ESQUILACHE
AQUASPORT
PAZ SOLAN
CASA ANDINA

MANZANILLA
SALAZAR
PAZ SOLAN
AV. BELEN
STA. MARGARITA
MAURTUA
ANGAMOS
OESTE
CLINICA ANGLO-AMERICANA
PUNTA SAL
OSAKA
BRAVO RESTOBAR
LA BAGUETTE
FELIPE PARDO Y ALIAGA
CAVENCIA

ÓVALO GUTIÉRREZ ★
To Miraflores

0   400 yds
0   400 m

© AVALON TRAVEL

1256, Lince, tel. 01/471-0117, http://museohn. unmsm.edu.pe, 9am-3pm Mon.-Fri., 9am-5pm Sat., 9am-1pm Sun., US$3) is a severely underfunded museum with an aging taxidermy collection that nevertheless offers a good introduction to the fauna of Peru. Ask for permission to see the storage area in the back, where thousands of stuffed birds are archived.

Museo Amano (Retiro 160, www.fundacionmuseoamano.org.pe, tel. 01/441-2909, 3pm-5pm by appointment only) has a small but interesting collection of 200 pre-Columbian ceramics, including a Nasca piece with a scene of human sacrifice, along with a range of textiles, which are the museum's specialty.

The **Museo Enrico Poli** (Lord Cochrane 466, tel. 01/422-2437 or 01/440-7100, 9am-4pm, by appointment only, US$12) is one of Lima's more intriguing private collections, with a huge range of textiles, gold and silver objects, and other artifacts. The owner, Enrico Poli, gives the tours personally and speaks Spanish only. Agencies often visit here with their own interpreters.

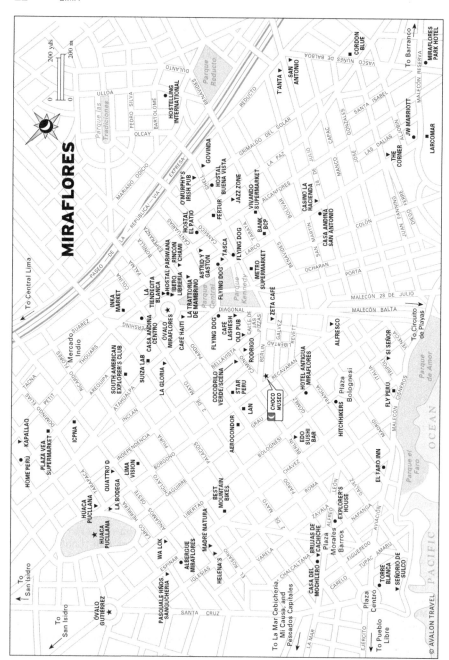

MIRAFLORES

200 yds
200 m

To Central Lima

To San Isidro

To San Isidro
To Pueblo Libre
To La Mar Cebichería, Mi Causa, and Pescados Capitales

To Barranco

PACIFIC OCEAN

© AVALON TRAVEL

MIRAFLORES PARK HOTEL
CORDON BLUE
SAN ANTONIO
T'ANTA
THE CORNER
LARCOMAR
JW MARRIOTT
CASINO LA HACIENDA
CASA ANDINA SAN ANTONIO
HOSTAL BUENA VISTA
GOVINDA
O'MURPHY'S IRISH PUB
FERTUR
JAZZ ZONE
VIVANDO SUPERMARKET
BANK BCP
FLYING DOG
TASCA
ASTRID Y GASTON
METRO SUPERMARKET
HOSTAL EL PATIO
RINCON CHAMI
HOSTAL PARIWANA
IBERO LIBRERIA
LA TRATTORIA DE MAMBRINO
ZETA CAFÉ
LA TIENDECITA BLANCA
INKA MARKET
CASA ANDINA CENTRO
OVALO MIRAFLORES
CAFÉ HAITI
CAFÉ LASHESH
OLD PUB
FLYING DOG
ALFRESCO
SI SEÑOR
HOSTELLING INTERNATIONAL
HOTEL ANTIGUA MIRAFLORES
RODRIGO
COCODRILO VERDE/SCENA
STAR PERU
CHOCO MUSEO
LAN
AEROCONDOR
Plaza Bolognesi
HITCHHIKERS
FLY PERU
EDO SUSHI BAR
EL FARO INN
SOUTH AMERICAN EXPLORER'S CLUB
SUIZA LAB
LA GLORIA
KAPALLAQ
HOME PERU
PLAZA VEA SUPERMARKET
ICPNA
QUATTRO D
LA BODEGA
LIMA VISION
HUACA PUCLLANA
HUACA PUCLLANA
BEST MOUNTAIN BIKES
MADRE NATURA
WA LOK
ALBERGUE MIRAFLORES
HELENA'S
EXPLORER'S HOUSE
BRUJAS DE CACHICHE
CASA DEL MOCHILERO
TORRE BLANCA
SEÑORIO DE SULCO
Plaza Centro
OVALO GUTIERREZ
PASQUALE HNOS. SANGUCHERIA
Plaza Morales Barros
Parque Reducto
Parque las Tradiciones
Parque Central
Parque Kennedy
Parque de Amor
Parque el Faro

Choco Museo

Chocolate lovers rejoice. The new **Choco Museo** (Berlin 375, tel. 01/445-9708, www.chocomuseo.com, 11am-7pm daily), only three blocks from Parque Kennedy, has hands-on workshops on how chocolate is made. Participants in the Beans to Bar class will get some theory about the cacao tree and harvesting before getting their hands dirty by roasting cacao beans and molding their own chocolate bars. There is also a workshop where you can make truffles. A two-hour workshop costs US$27.50 for adults and US$19.50 for children.

Bosque El Olivar

Tucked away in a residential area of San Isidro is **Bosque El Olivar,** one of the city's nicest green spaces with a history dating back more than 450 years. The 23-hectare park is home to some 1,500 olive trees that can be traced to saplings first brought to Lima by Spaniards in 1560. This is a good spot to go to take a break from the city's modern rush. San Isidro's

municipal library (República 420, tel. 01/513-9000) is located in the park.

BARRANCO

The bohemian neighborhood of Barranco isn't known for museums, but there have been a couple new openings that may interest those who like contemporary art and photography. **Museo Pedro de Osma** (San Pedro de Osma 423, tel. 01/467-0141, www.museopedrodeosma.org, 10am-6pm Tues.-Sun., US$7) holds an exquisite private collection of colonial art and furniture; the building is one of Barranco's oldest mansions and is worth a peek just for that reason. On the same block is Peruvian fashion photographer Mario Testino's **Mate** (San Pedro de Osma 409, tel. 01/251-7755, 11am-8pm Tues.-Sat., 11am-6pm Sun., US$7) which has a revolving exhibit of his work and a nice café in the back. A better option is the **Museo de Arte Contemporáneo** (Grau 1511, tel. 01/652-5100, 10am-5pm Tues.-Sun., US$5), with a nice selection of contemporary paintings from international and Peruvian artists, as well as

Bosque El Olivar in San Isidro

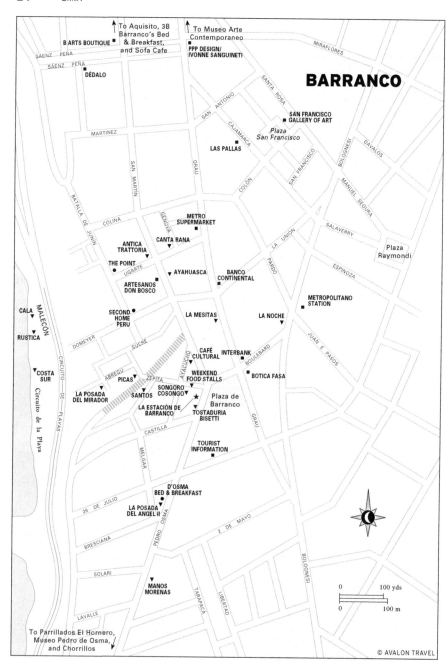

To Aquisito, 3B
Barranco's Bed
& Breakfast,
and Sofa Cafe

To Museo Arte
Contemporaneo

B ARTS BOUTIQUE

SÁENZ PEÑA

SÁENZ PEÑA

PPP DESIGN/
IVONNE SANGUINETI

DÉDALO

MIRAFLORES

BARRANCO

MARTINEZ

SAN ANTONIO

SANTA ROSA

CAJAMARCA

SAN FRANCISCO
GALLERY OF ART

Plaza
San Francisco

LAS PALLAS

GRAU

COLÓN

SAN FRANCISCO

BOLOGNESI

DAVALOS

MANUEL SEGURA

SAN MARTIN

BATALLA DE JUNIN

COLINA

METRO
SUPERMARKET

GENOVA

CANTA RANA

ANTICA
TRATTORIA

THE POINT

UGARTE

AYAHUASCA

ARTESANOS
DON BOSCO

BANCO
CONTINENTAL

LA UNIÓN

PARDO

SALAVERRY

ESPINOZA

Plaza
Raymondi

CALA

MALECÓN

RUSTICA

SECOND
HOME
PERU

LA MESITAS

LA NOCHE

METROPOLITANO
STATION

DOMEYER

SÚCRE

CIRCUITO DE PLAYAS

Circuito de la Playa

COSTA
SUR

ABREGU

PICAS

ZEPITA

LA POSADA
DEL MIRADOR

SANTOS

AYACUCHO

CAFÉ
CULTURAL

INTERBANK

WEEKEND
FOOD STALLS

SONGORO
COSONGO

LA ESTACIÓN DE
BARRANCO

CASTILLA

BOULEVARD

BOTICA FASA

★ Plaza de
Barranco

TOSTADURIA
BISETTI

JUAN E. PASOS

GRAU

MELGAR

TOURIST
INFORMATION

D'OSMA
BED & BREAKFAST

28 DE JULIO

LA POSADA
DEL ANGEL II

PEDRO OSMA

2 DE MAYO

BRESCIANA

SOLARI

BOLOGNESI

MANOS
MORENAS

TARAPACA

LIBERTAD

LAVALLE

To Parrillados El Hornero,
Museo Pedro de Osma,
and Chorrillos

0		100 yds
0		100 m

© AVALON TRAVEL

modernist sculptures located on its terrace. It also offers classes in painting, theater, dance, and music for adults and children. Finally, there is a small exhibit on electricity in Lima at the **Museo de la Electricidad** (San Pedro de Osma 105, tel. 01/477-6577, 9am-5pm daily, free). A restored electric tram (US$2.75), which used to connect Barranco to Miraflores and Lima, runs down the street on Sunday.

EASTERN LIMA
Museo de Oro
Monterrico, an upscale suburb in eastern Lima that is often sunny when the rest of the city is covered in fog, is known for its **Museo de Oro** (Molina 1110, Monterrico, tel. 01/345-1271, www.museoroperu.com.pe 10:30am-6pm daily, US$12). This fabulous collection of gold pieces was one of Lima's must-see attractions until 2001, when a scandal broke alleging that many of the prize pieces were fakes. Newspapers pointed the finger at the sons of museum founder Miguel Mujica Gallo, whom the newspapers accused of selling the originals and replacing them with imitations. The family countered, saying false pieces were bought by mistake, and that Mujica Gallo died of sadness in the process. Only true gold pieces are on display now at the museum, but the museum continues to suffer from a credibility problem. Gold pieces include spectacular funerary masks, ceremonial knives (*tumis*), a huge set of golden arms, exquisite figurines, and crowns studded with turquoise. It is a huge potpourri of gold, with little explanation in English, bought over decades from tomb raiders who work over Moche, Nasca, Sicán, and Chimú sites. Other objects of interest include a Nasca poncho made of parrot feathers and a Moche skull that was fitted, postmortem, with purple quartz teeth. Almost as impressive is the **Arms Museum** upstairs, which is a terrifying assemblage of thousands of weapons, ranging from samurai swords and medieval harquebuses to Hitler paraphernalia.

Museo de la Nación
Peru's largest museum, and cheaper to see than the private collections, is **Museo de la Nación** (Javier Prado Este 2465, tel. 01/476-9873, 9am-6pm Tues.-Sun., US$4, US$3 students), in the east Lima suburb of San Borja. Though criticized for its rambling organization, this museum, which is located in the same building as the Ministry of Culture, has a great chronological layout, making it perhaps Lima's most understandable and educational museum. There are three levels of exhibits showcasing Peru's entire archaeological history, from Chavín stone carvings and Paracas weavings all the way to the Inca. There are good models of Machu Picchu, the Nasca Lines, and the Lords of Sipán tomb excavated near Chiclayo in 1987, one of the great finds of Latin American archaeology. On the sixth floor is a chilling photo exhibit called *Yuyanapaq*, which means "to remember" in Quechua. The exhibit documents Peru's internal conflict between Shining Path rebels and state security forces that claimed almost 70,000 lives in the 1980s and 1990s. A permanent home for the exhibit will be the **Lugar de la Memoria** museum, which is currently under construction on a lot donated by Miraflores and overlooking the Pacific.

OUTSIDE LIMA
Pachacámac
This extensive complex of adobe pyramids, 31 kilometers south of Lima in the Lurín Valley, was the leading pilgrimage center on the central coast and home to the most feared and respected oracle in the Andes. The name of Pachacámac in Quechua translates to "Lord of the World." Both the Huari and local Inca empires respected the oracle, adding to its prestige with additional buildings and consulting it for important decisions.

During his imprisonment at Cajamarca, the Inca Atahualpa complained bitterly because the oracle had falsely predicted he would be victorious against the Spaniards. But Hernando Pizarro was so intrigued by Atahualpa's reports of gold at the oracle that he and a troop of Spanish soldiers rode here from Cajamarca in three weeks. Pushing aside the priests, Pizarro strode to the upmost level of

Pachacámac ruins, outside Lima

© BEATRICE VELARDE/PROMPERU

the stepped pyramid. He describes a cane-and-mud house at the top, with a door strangely decorated with turquoise, crystals, and corals. Inside the dark space was a roughly shaped wooden idol. "Seeing the filth and mockery of the idol," Pizarro wrote, "we went out to ask why they thought highly of something so dirty and ugly."

What can be seen today is the idol itself (probably a replica) in the on-site museum and excavations of the main temples and huge pyramids, which have revealed ramps and entranceways. From the top of the Temple of the Sun there is an impressive view of Lima's well-organized shantytown, Villa El Salvador, and the Pacific Coast. The Palacio de Las Mamacuña, the enclosure for holy women built by the Inca, can be seen with a guide only (US$6 for an English-speaking tour of the entire site). On the way to the ruins, you will pass **Reserva Pantanos de Villa** at Km 18 on the Panamericana Sur. There is a surprisingly diverse range of ducks and other migratory aquatic birds here that lures bird-watchers.

The easiest way to see the Pachacámac ruins and the corresponding **museum** (http://pachacamac.perucultural.org.pe) is with an agency tour from Lima. Buses marked "Pachacámac" leave from Montevideo and Ayacucho in central Lima and can be picked up at the Primavera Bridge along the Panamericana Sur (US$4 taxi ride to the bridge from Miraflores). Ask to be dropped off at *las ruinas,* as the town of Pachacámac is farther along.

San Pedro de Casta and Marcahuasi

Marcahuasi is a strange set of rock formations on the high plains above Lima that has attracted a range of theories as to their origins, from simple wind erosion to the work of ancient cultures or aliens. The rocks are shaped like people and animals, inspiring names like the Frog, the Indian, the Three Virgins, and the Turtle. Marcahuasi is set amid attractive country scenery and, along with the nearby charming town of San Pedro, makes for a great weekend outing from Lima. To get here, catch a bus from Avenida Grau in Lima (near Plaza Grau in the center) and travel 1.5 hours to **Chosica,** a resort town 860 meters above sea level that is popular with those trying to escape Lima's fog belt. There are plenty of budget and nicer lodging options here. From Chosica's Parque Echenique, buses leave to San Pedro, a beautiful four- or five-hour trip that climbs to 3,750 meters above sea level. There is a **hostel** (US$8 pp) in the main square, along with restaurants and a tourist information office. Marcahuasi, at 4,100 meters above sea level, is a three-kilometer 1.5-hour hike; donkeys (US$6) can be rented. The entry fee is US$5.

Entertainment and Events

NIGHTLIFE
Central Lima
There are a few night options in the center of Lima, and you should take a taxi to and from each one. On the Plaza San Martín is **El Estadio Futbol Club** (Nícolas de Piérola 926, tel. 01/428-8866, www.estadio.com.pe, 1pm-11pm Mon.-Thurs., 1pm-3am Fri.-Sat., noon-3pm Sun.), a soccer lover's paradise bedecked with *fútbol* paraphernalia.

One of the largest and best *peñas* in Lima is **Brisas del Titicaca** (Tarapacá 168, previously Wakulski, near block 1 of Brasil and Plaza Bolognesi, tel. 01/715-6960, www.brisasdeltiticaca.com, Tues.-Sat., cover US$18). Foreigners come on Thursday nights for an extraordinary exhibition of dance and music from around Peru (9:30pm-1:30am Thurs.). Those who want to see the same dances, and dance a lot themselves, should come 10pm-2:30am weekend nights, when mainly Peruvians party. This is a safe neighborhood and is an easy taxi ride from Miraflores.

San Isidro
If you have come to Avenida Conquistadores for dinner, there are a few nightlife options that also serve light dinners along this strip. A popular choice is **Bravo Restobar** (Conquistadores 1005, tel. 01/221-5700, www.bravorestobar. com, 12:30pm-1am Mon.-Thurs., 12:30pm-2am Fri.-Sat., US$15-20), a swanky wine bar that fills with Lima's hip 30-something crowd most nights of the week. It has a good selection of pisco cocktails, including *lúcuma* sour and grape sour.

Miraflores
The nightlife in Miraflores is more spread out and harder to find than in the neighboring district of Barranco. And that is precisely why many a traveler ends up at **Calle de las Pizzas** (The Street of the Pizzas), a seedy row of pizza-and-sangria joints right in front of Parque Kennedy. But there are many other options.

If you're looking for some live music, you won't be disappointed with **Jazz Zone** (La Paz 656, tel. 01/241-8139, www.jazzzoneperu.com, cover US$8-12), where some of the best local music in town can be found. Music normally gets going at around 10pm. Sit back and enjoy with a Cusqueña beer or pisco sour.

For cocktails and music, swing around to Francisco de Paula Camino Street to **Cocodrilo Verde** (Francisco de Paula Camino 226, tel. 01/242-7583, www.cocodriloverde.com, 9pm-midnight Tues.-Wed., 9pm-12:30am Thurs., 9pm-2am Fri.-Sat., cover US$5-15). Next door, **Scena Restaurante** (Francisco Paula de Camino 280, tel. 01/445-9688, www.scena. com.pe, 12:30pm-4pm and 7:30pm-12:30am Mon.-Sat., US$10-15) has a great wine list and a rotating art exhibit. On the same street is **Bizarro** (Francisco De Paula Camino 22, tel. 01/446-3508, www.bizarrobar.com, 9pm-3am Tues., 9pm-5am Wed.-Sun.), an upscale dance club.

A popular winter drink sold by street vendors in Peru is the herbal-based *emoliente,* with a history dating to colonial Lima. Now there is a place that serves *emolientes* with Peru's national drink, pisco—a block from Parque Kennedy, newly opened **La Emolientería** (Oscar

Gay and Lesbian Lima

Though smaller than in other Latin American capitals, Lima's gay scene is growing, with a few great new discos and bars. There are a number of websites on gay Peru, but the best and most up-to-date information is **GayCities** (www.lima.gaycities.com). This site, written in English, has travel tips, a chat room, links, and an opinionated listing of gay and lesbian bars, discos, saunas, cruising spots, and even retirement options. Other sites include **Peru Es Gay** (www.peruesgay.com) and **Gay Peru** (www.gayperu.com).

Gay and lesbian discos do not start swinging until 1am and continue until the wee hours of the morning. Entry is typically free on weekday nights and goes up after midnight on weekends. Miraflores's hippest, classiest gay and lesbian disco is **Legendaris** (Berlin 363, www.gayperu.com/legendaris, 11pm-late Wed.-Sun., US$4.50 before midnight, US$6 after), which opened in January 2004 with extravagant decor, a great sound system, and room for 350. The flamboyant **Downtown Vale Todo** (Pasaje Los Pinos 160, Miraflores, tel. 01/444-6436, www.peruesgay.com/downtownvaletodo, 10:30pm-late Wed.-Sun., US$4 Fri.-Sat.) is still open despite some citizens' efforts to shut it down. This disco attracts a younger crowd, with drag queen performances and a cruising bar on an upper deck.

One of the only options in central Lima is **Sagitario** (Wilson 869, tel. 01/424-4383, www.gayperu.com/sagitariodisco, daily, free except after midnight on weekends), one of Lima's original gay-only bars. The neighborhood is sketchy at night, so travel by taxi. **Avenida 13** (Manuel Segura 270, off block 15 of Arequipa, tel. 01/265-3694) is a gay and lesbian dance club that is women-only on Friday.

Gay-friendly hotels include **Hostal de las Artes** in the center, **Hostel Domeyer** in Barranco, and **Aparthotel San Martín** in Miraflores. Other options can be found at **Purple Roofs** (www.purpleroofs.com).

Benavides 598, tel. 01/446-3431, noon-1am Sun.-Thurs., noon-3am Fri.-Sat., US$10) is a brightly lit *restobar.* On a chilly Lima night, try an *emoliente* with pisco to warm up. **Huaringas** (Bolognesi 460, tel. 01/466-6536, www.brujasdecachiche.com.pe, noon-4:30pm and 7pm-midnight Mon.-Sat., 12:30pm-4:30pm Sun.) is rumored to have the best pisco sours in town. Get there early and try the strawberry, passion fruit, and grape sours.

There are several British-style pubs in Miraflores, good for drinking draft ale and playing darts; the classic is **Murphy's Irish Pub** (Schell 627, tel. 01/650-8267, 6pm-2am daily), with darts and a pool table. For a typical American sports bar there's **The Corner Sports Bar and Grill** (Larco 1207, tel. 01/444-0220, noon-12:30am Mon.-Thurs., noon-2am Fri.-Sat., noon-11:30pm Sun., US$8), whose 26 TVs broadcast international sports games.

There is always something happening at **Larcomar** (Malecón de la Reserva 610, tel. 01/625-4343, www.larcomar.com), the ocean-front mall at the end of Avenida Larco. Even those who dislike malls are impressed with this public space, buried in the cliff side and overlooking the Pacific. Lima's hottest and most expensive disco, **Aura** (Larcomar 236, tel. 01/242-5516, www.aura.com.pe, 10:30pm-7am Thurs., 2:30am-7am Fri., 10:30pm-7am-Sat., cover varies), is here.

Barranco

The most happening neighborhood for nightlife any day of the week is Barranco. There are several spots close to Barranco's main plaza, including a number of bars and dance clubs on the Sanchez Carrión walkway. The best spot on the boulevard is **La Noche** (Bolognesi 307, tel. 01/247-1012, www.lanoche.com.pe, 7pm-1am Mon.-Tues., 7pm-3am Wed.-Sat., US$6-9), which has good live music. Tables are set on different levels to look down on a range of performances.

Located in a mansion built in the late 19th century, **Ayahuasca** (San Martín 130, tel. 9810-24126, www.ayahuascarestobar.com, 8pm-3am Mon.-Sat., US$10-15) is as much fun for its drinks as it is for its decor. Named after the hallucinogenic drink, Ayahuasca's interior is inspired by Amazonian shamanism and the bright colors of Andean designs while maintaining the villa's 19th-century feel. Ayahuasca serves an excellent selection of pisco-based cocktails, including the Ayahuasca sour. It also has a good menu of appetizers and main dishes.

Overlooking Barranco's romantic *puente de suspiros* (Bridge of Sighs) is the popular **Santos** (Zepita 203, tel. 01/247-4609, 5pm-late daily), with a long, slender patio that fills up on weekends. On the other side of the bridge is **Picas** (Bajada de Banos 340, tel. 01/247-6150, www.picas.com.pe, 8pm-late daily), which serves up cocktails.

For a glass of wine and some excellent *trova* music, head to **La Posada del Angel II** (Pedro de Osma 218, tel. 01/251-3778, 7pm-late daily). There are two other locations on the same street, each with baroque decor and a large angel statue in the entrance. For a view overlooking the Pacific is **La Posada del Mirador** (Ermita 104, tel. 01/256-1796, noon-midnight daily). This is a good place to have an early pisco sour while watching the sunset.

Barranco is full of *peñas* (live *criollo* music clubs) that make for a rowdy night out among locals. **La Candelaría** (Bolognesi 292, tel. 01/247-2941, www.lacandelariaperu.com, 9pm-2am Fri.-Sun., US$15) is a comfortable *peña* where spectators do not stay seated for long. With a slightly older crowd, **La Estación de Barranco** (Pedro de Osma 112, tel. 01/247-0344, 7pm-2am daily, no cover) is a nice place to hear *música criolla* in the digs of an old train station. The hippest, but still authentic, *peña* is **Peña del Carajo** (Catalino Miranda 158, tel. 01/247-7023, www.delcarajo.com.pe, 10pm-4am Fri.-Sat., no cover).

CINEMAS

Lima has more cinemas than the rest of the country combined. Most foreign movies are

© RYAN DUBÉ

Santos bar in Barranco, overlooking the *puente de suspiros*

shown in two theaters, one showing in their original language with subtitles and another dubbed, so be sure to double-check when buying your ticket. Children's movies are often dubbed. Film listings are posted in *El Comercio* (www.elcomercio.pe) newspaper as well as the websites of the main cinema companies: **Cinemark** (www.cinemark-peru.com), **Cineplanet** (www.cineplanet.com.pe) and **UVK Multicines** (www.uvkmulticines.com).

The *Centro Cultural PUCP* (Camino Real 1075, tel. 01/616-1616, www.cultural.pucp.edu.pe), in San Isidro, hosts several film festivals throughout the year. Its biggest show is in August with the increasingly well-known **Lima Latin American Film Festival** (www.festivaldelima.com).

In Miraflores alone there are at least three multiplexes showing both Hollywood and Latin American movies: **Cineplanet Alcázar** (Santa Cruz 814, Ovalo Gutiérrez, Miraflores, tel. 01/421-8208, www.cineplanet.com.pe, US$7), **El Pacífico 12** (José Pardo 121, Miraflores, tel. 01/445-6990, US$5.50), and **Multicines Larcomar** (Larcomar mall, at end of Larco, tel. 01/446-7336, www.uvk-multicines.com, US$5). A smaller recommended theater is in the **Centro Cultural Ricardo Palma** (Larco 770, Miraflores, tel. 01/617-7266). In central Lima is **Cineplanet Centro** (Jr. de la Union 819, tel. 01/428-8460, www.cineplanet.com.pe, US$2, US$3.50 Mon.-Wed.).

PERFORMING ARTS

For the most up-to-date listing of cultural events, pick up the monthly *Lima Cultura: Agenda Cultural* (www.limacultura.pe), which is available free in most museums and cultural centers, or view its website. *El Comercio* (www.elcomercioperu.pe) newspaper also has complete listings.

Lima's performing arts scene got a big boost with the recent opening of the **Gran Teatro Nacional** (Javier Prado Este 2225, San Borja, tel. 01/715-3659, prices vary). Located beside the **Museo de la Nación** and Peru's national library, this is a multipurpose theater that has concerts by Peru's National Symphony Orchestra and Peruvian folk musicals. There are also operas, ballets, and international jazz. Renowned Peruvian tenor Juan Diego Flórez has performed here a few times. Show times vary, so your best bet is to pick up the bimonthly program at the theater or visit **Teleticket**, located in the Wong and Metro supermarkets. Another option for performing arts is **Teatro Segura** (Huancavelica 265, central Lima, tel. 01/426-7189), one of the oldest theater houses in Latin America.

Theater productions, always in Spanish, can be seen at **Centro Cultural de España** (Natalio Sánchez 181, Sta. Beatriz, tel. 01/330-0412, www.ccelima.org), **Centro Cultural PUCP** (Camino Real 1075, San Isidro, tel. 01/616-1616, http://cultural.pucp.edu.pe), **Teatro Canout** (Petit Thouars 4550, Miraflores, tel. 01/593-7654, www.teatrocanout.com.pe), **Teatro Marsano** (General Suárez 409, Miraflores, tel. 01/620-6400, www.teatroplaza.com), **Alianza Francesa** (Arequipa 4595, tel. 01/241-7014, www.alianzafrancesalima.edu.pe), and **Teatro Británico** (Bellavista 531, Miraflores, tel. 01/447-1135, www.britanico.edu.pe), which occasionally has plays in English. Tickets are normally purchased at the box office for only US$8-12.

Other frequent cultural events, such as films, concerts, and expositions, are held at the **Instituto Cultural Peruano Norteamericano** (tel. 01/706-7000, www.icpna.edu.pe), with a location in central Lima (Cusco 446) and Miraflores (Angamos Oeste 106); and the **Centro Cultural Ricardo Palma** (Larco 770, Miraflores, tel. 01/446-3959).

CASINOS

Lima is overflowing with casinos, though the most reputable ones tend to be in the major hotels. Some casinos open in the evenings and close around dawn; others are open 24 hours daily. Regardless, they usually offer free drinks and food to those who are betting. In San Isidro there's a casino in the upscale **Los Delfines Hotel** (Los Eucaliptos 555, tel. 01/215-7000). In Miraflores, there is the **Stellaris Casino** at the Marriott (Malecón de la Reserva 615, across the street from Larcomar, tel. 01/217-7000), and the popular **Atlantic City** (Benavides 430, tel. 01/705-4400, www.acity.com.pe) and **Fiesta** (Benavides 509, tel. 01/610-4150, www.fiesta-casino.pe).

SPECTATOR SPORTS

Lima is a great place to catch a **soccer game,** either at the recently remodeled Estadio Nacional along the Vía Expresa and 28 de Julio or at the Estadio Monumental Lolo Fernández in the Molina neighborhood. Games happen mostly on Wednesday, Saturday, and Sunday, and prices and locations are published two days beforehand in the newspaper. The two biggest teams in Lima are Alianza Lima and Club Universitario, called simply "La U." Tickets run US$5-9 and can usually be bought the same day for nonchampionship matches. Tickets are bought at the stadium, and at TeleTicket counters in the Wong and Metro supermarkets. The cheap tickets, in the far ends of the stadium, can get rowdy, especially during games between rival Lima teams.

Bullfighting takes place at the Plaza de Acho (Hualgayoc 332, tel. 01/481-1467) near the center of Lima from late October to the first week of December. It's a centuries-old tradition that coincides with Lima's biggest festival, El Señor de los Milagros. Tickets for the Sunday afternoon events range US$30-100 for a two-hour contest featuring world-class bullfighters from Spain and Peru. Tickets are sold at TeleTicket counters in the Wong and Metro supermarkets.

Cockfights, traditionally part of *criollo* culture, are weekend events at various *peñas* and popular in the working-class neighborhoods on the outskirts of Lima. **Horse races** can be seen at the **Jockey Club of Peru** (El Derby s/n, puerta 3, Hipódromo de Monterrico, tel. 01/610-3000, www.jcp.org.pe). To watch American football or European soccer, head to **The Corner Sports Bar and Grill** (Larco 1207, tel. 01/444-0220, 11am-3am daily).

FESTIVALS

Lima's biggest festival is **El Señor de los Milagros** (The Lord of Miracles), which draws as many as 500,000 people on its main days, October 18 and 28; the festival is accompanied by bullfights at Plaza de Acho. The processions begin in central Lima at **Iglesia Las Nazarenas** (Tacna and Huancavelica), which was built atop a wall where an African slave painted an image of Christ in the 17th century. The wall was the only thing left standing after a 1755 earthquake, prompting this annual festival in October, the month when Lima's worst earthquakes have traditionally struck. To this day a brotherhood of priests of mainly African descent care for the image, which some anthropologists say is related to the pre-Hispanic cult of Pachacámac.

Other good festivals include **Lima's anniversary** (Jan. 18), the **Feast of Santa Rosa de Lima** (Aug. 30), and **Día de la Canción Criolla** (Creole Music Day, Oct. 31), when *peñas* hold a variety of concerts around the city.

Peruvian *paso* horse competitions are held in the Lurín Valley south of Lima and are highly recommended. These include the Peruvian Paso Horse Competition in February, a national competition in Mamacona in April, and the Amancaes competition, also in Mamacona, in July.

Shopping

Lima is the clearinghouse for handicrafts produced in places like Huancayo and Ayacucho, and they are sold with a considerable markup. There is a huge range of goods, from cheap tourist-oriented items to those sold in boutique shops, but bargaining is always an option. Several American-style malls have been built in Lima, most notably the cliff-side Larcomar at the end of Avenida Larco and under the Parque Salazar.

HANDICRAFTS

In **Pueblo Libre,** an excellent crafts markets with a cause is **La Casa de la Mujer Artesana Manuela Ramos** (Juan Pablo Fernandini 1550, 15th block of Brasil, Pueblo Libre, tel. 01/423-8840, www.casadelamujerartesana.com, 9am-5pm Mon.-Fri.). Proceeds from this market benefit women's programs across Peru.

The largest crafts markets are in **Miraflores**, in blocks 52 and 54 of Petit Thouars. Market after market is filled with alpaca clothing, silver jewelry, ceramics, and textiles from all over the country. **Mercado Indio** (Petit Thouars 5245, 10am-6pm daily) and **Indian Market** (Petit Thouars 5321, 9am-8pm daily) are the best of the lot, with nicely presented stalls and wide selections. Nearby is a **Manos Peruanas** (Plaza Artesanal, Petit Thouars 5411, tel. 01/242-9726, 10:30am-7:30pm daily), with a contemporary line of handcrafted silver earrings, necklaces, and bracelets. Other huge, cheap crafts markets are **Feria Artesanal** (Av. Marina, Pueblo Libre, 10am-6pm daily) on the way to the airport—every taxi knows it—or in central Lima across from Iglesia Santo Domingo, at the intersection of Camaná and Superunda.

In **Parque Kennedy,** you can find rows of Peruvian artists selling their paintings of

Talk with artists and peruse their work in Parque Kennedy.

© RYAN DUBÉ

Lima's colonial past and traditional life in the Andes. The artists are normally out on the weekends. Crafts are also normally sold in the parquet, sometimes by indigenous men and women traveling from Cusco and other Andean towns.

Miraflores's other main shopping strips are in the area next to Parque Kennedy that includes La Paz, Schell, and Diez Canseco Streets. The reasonably priced **Hecho a Mano** (Diez Canseco 298, 10am-5pm Mon.-Sat.) has a high-quality selection of crafts from all parts of Peru, especially Ayacucho. Another plaza at Diez Canseco 380 is filled with jewelry shops, and a wide selection of baby alpaca sweaters can be found at Diez Canseco 378.

For a more upmarket shopping experience, visit the hugely popular **Larcomar** (Malecón de la Reserva 610, tel. 01/625-4343, www.larcomar.com, 11am-10pm daily), an elegant open-air mall dug under Miraflores's Parque Salazar and perched over the ocean. Upscale alpaca clothing stores, the finest of which is **Kuna** (www.alpaca111.com), as well as cafés, a sushi restaurant, bars, a disco, and a 12-screen cinema are just a few of the businesses here. An excellent place for high-quality jewelry and silver decorations is **Ilaria** (tel. 01/242-8084, www.ilariainternational.com) located on the second level.

The most sophisticated range of handicrafts in Lima can be found in **Barranco.** The high-end gallery **Las Pallas** (Cajamarca 212, tel. 01/477-4629, 10am-7pm Mon.-Sat.) has exquisite Amazon textiles, tapestries, and carved gourds from Huancayo, as well as colonial ceramics from Cusco; prices run US$30-800. Another good option for high-end crafts and art is **Dédalo** (Sáenz Pena 295, Barranco, tel. 01/477-0562, 11am-9pm Tues.-Sun.).

Artesanos Don Bosco (San Martín 135, Barranco, tel. 01/713-1344, www.artesanosdonbosco.pe, 10:30am-7pm Tues.-Sun.) was started in the 1970s by a Catholic priest in the Andean town of Chacas, near Huaraz. The initiative aimed to give young people working skills to escape poverty through artisan crafts. Today, the organization has expanded,

with offices in the United States, Cusco, and Barranco. High-end work is on display and includes contemporary furniture, ceramics, blown glass, weavings, and stone sculptures. For Ayacucho crafts, try **Museo-Galería Popular de Ayacucho** (Pedro de Osma 116, tel. 01/247-0599).

Sáenz Peña is the street for contemporary art. There are numerous galleries with artwork that is mostly modern and includes paintings, photography, and sculpture. Check out **Lucía de la Puente Galeria de Arte** (Sáenz Peña 206, tel. 01/477-9740, www.gluciadelapuente.com, 11am-8pm Mon.-Fri., 3pm-8pm Sat.), in a large old mansion; **PPPP Design** (Grau 810, tel. 01/247-7976, www.ppppdesign.com, 10am-6:30pm Mon.-Fri., 10am-4pm Fri.); or **Yvonne Sanguineti** (Grau 810, tel. 01/247-2999, 11am-8pm Mon.-Sat.).

OPEN-AIR MARKET

There are several busy open-air markets in Lima where you can find stands full of fresh produce, meats, and seafood. These markets are still bursting with shoppers, even though large modern grocery stores have sprung up across the capital. One of the reasons is that they are often cheaper, while another is perhaps the personal relationships that store owners form with their clients. The best market to visit is the **Mercado 1** (Av. Paseo de la República, 6:30am-9pm daily), in the Surquillo neighborhood, located right across the bridge from Miraflores on Ricardo Palma and the Vía Expresa. Many of Peru's top chefs are known to shop here.

CAMPING EQUIPMENT

If you need to buy outdoor gear, you will pay a premium in Peru, and your only options are Lima, Huaraz, and Cusco. Varying qualities of white gas, or *bencina blanca,* can be bought at hardware stores across Peru, so test your stove before you depart. Gas canisters are available only at specialty outdoor stores.

Miraflores has several camping stores: **Alpamayo** (Larco 345, tel. 01/445-1671, www.alpamayoexploracion.pe, 9am-1pm and 2:30pm-7pm Mon.-Fri., 9am-1pm Sat.) sells tents, backpacks, sleeping mats, boots, rock shoes, climbing gear, water filters, MSR stoves, and more. Similar items are found at **Camping Center** (Benavides 1620 Miraflores, tel. 01/242-1779, www.campingperu.com, 10am-7pm Mon.-Fri., 10am-1pm Sat.). **Todo Camping E.I.R.L.** (Angamos Oeste 350, Miraflores, tel. 01/242-1318, 10am-8pm Mon.-Fri.) also sells more technical equipment like crampons and higher-end fuel stoves.

BOOKSTORES

The best bookstore in central Lima is **El Virrey** (Paseo los Escribanos 115, tel. 01/427-5080, www.elvirrey.com, 10am-9pm Mon.-Sat.). If you are looking for specialty books in science, history, or sociology, this is the place to find them. The store also has a new location in Miraflores (Bolognesi 510, Miraflores, tel. 01/444-4141, 9am-8:30pm Mon.-Sat., 11am-7pm Sun.).

Additionally, there are several bookstores, or *librerías,* in Miraflores with good English and other foreign language sections. Despite its humble door, **SBS** (Angamos Oeste 301, tel. 01/206-4900, www.sbs.com.pe, 9am-7pm Mon.-Fri., 9am-noon Sat.) has the best collection of English-language guidebooks. Its storefront on Parque Kennedy goes by the name **Ibero Librería** (Larco 199, tel. 01/206-4900, 10am-8pm daily) and has an excellent selection of English-language books as well as helpful staff. **Crisol** (Santa Cruz 816, Óvalo Gutierrez, tel. 01/221-1010, www.crisol.com.pe, 10am-11pm Sun.-Thurs., 10am-midnight Fri.-Sat.) is a huge glassy bookshop in the same mall as the Cineplant Alcázar. Other options are **Zeta** (Comandante Espinar 219, tel. 01/446-5139, www.zetabook.com, 9am-9pm Mon.-Sat.) and **Delta Bookstore Librería** (Larco 970).

Lima also hosts an **International Book Festival** (www.fillima.com.pe) at the end of July, which has thousands of books for sale as well as readings by authors and other cultural events. See the website for future schedules and programs. **International newspapers** are available from Miraflores street vendors in front of Café Haiti by Parque Kennedy.

Recreation

CYCLING

One way to see Lima is on a bicycle, either in a tour or setting out on your own. **Bike Tours of Lima** (Bolívar 150, Miraflores, tel. 01/445-3172, www.biketoursoflima.com) leads day excursions around Lima's bay area and through the colonial center. **Peru Bike** (Punta Sal D7, Surco, 01/260-8225, www.perubike.com) also does city tours as well as mountain biking trips just outside of Lima in the Pachacámac valley, and multiday tours in other parts of Peru. You can also rent a bike for a few hours from **Mirabici,** a municipal program that has a stand just outside the Larcomar shopping center in Miraflores. **BiciCentro** (Av. San Luis 2906, tel. 01/475-2645), in San Borja, is good for repairs and services.

BIRD-WATCHING

With an early start, there are several doable bird-watching day trips from Lima. **Pantanos de Villa** is a 396-hectare protected marsh within Lima's city limits. Here, you can see over 130 coastal marsh species, and the area is accessible by public transportation. For guaranteed sightings of the Humboldt penguin, your best option is the **Pucusana** fishing village. Public transportation also covers this route.

The updated edition of *Birds of Peru,* which has a forward by Peru's first environment minister, Antonio Brack, is an excellent bird-watching guide. The website of **PromPeru** (www.perubirdingroutes.com) is also chock-full of good information. To make your trip more efficient and learn more, you'll probably want to contact a guide. Princeton-trained biologist Thomas Valqui's company, **Gran Perú** (tel. 01/344-1701, www.granperu.com), leads a variety of scheduled tours and can also coordinate day trips and private trips. Swedish ornithologist Gunnar Engblom's agency, **Kolibri Expeditions** (tel. 01/273-7246, www.kolibriexpeditions.com), offers regular day expeditions in the Lima area.

COOKING

For those familiar with Lima's culinary delights, it should come as no surprise that it hosts a cooking school licensed by **Cordon Bleu** (Nuñez de Balboa 530, Miraflores, tel. 01/617-8300, www.cordonbleuperu.edu.pe, prices vary by course). The various classes include short-term seminars on Peruvian food, international food, and even desserts. Another option is the hotel and restaurant management school **Cenfotur** (Pedro Martinto 320, Barranco, tel. 01/319-8000, www.cenfotur.com), whose workshop classes also feature cocktail making and wine-tasting. At either of these institutions you will have to make special arrangements for English-speaking classes.

HORSEBACK RIDING

Check out **Cabalgatas** (tel. 9753-49004, www.cabalgatas.com.pe, from US$45), an option for riding Peruvian *paso* horses near Mamacona, the town where the *paso* horse competitions are held each year. They lead interesting excursions around the ceremonial center of Pachacámac.

PARAGLIDING

First-time visitors to Miraflores, promenading the *malecón*, are sometimes surprised to find a paraglider just meters above their heads, zipping back and forth along the oceanfront bluffs. Although the thrill is short-lived, paragliding does offer an excellent alternative viewpoint of Lima. One recommended operator is **Peru Fly** (Jorge Chávez 658, Miraflores, tel. 9930-86795, www.perufly.com), which organizes flights in Lima and Paracas and also offers six-day basic-training courses.

SCUBA

There are no coral reefs on Peru's Pacific coast, but agencies do offer interesting dives. **AguaSport** (Conquistadores 805, San Isidro, tel. 01/221-1548, www.aquasportperu.com) rents all equipment for snorkeling and scuba diving. Standard scuba day trips from Lima include a 30-meter wall dive at Pucusana, an 18-meter dive to a nearby sunken ship, or diving with sea lions at Islas Palomino off Lima. Two dives are US$95, or US$55 if you have your own equipment. This agency rents a range of aquatic and off-road equipment.

SEA KAYAKING

For those who like to get out on the water but aren't surfers, there's always sea kayaking. **Peru Sea Kayaking** (San Borja Norte 1241-201, San Borja tel. 9978-99752, www.peruseakayaking.com, from US$70 pp) is a professionally run operation, with new equipment, that takes passengers out on the Pacific anywhere between Ancón and Cerro Azul.

SURFING

For surfers, you don't need to go far to catch a wave. In Miraflores you'll find dozens of surfers in the waters at the Makaha and Waikiki beaches, which are good for beginners. The bigger breaks are at La Herradura in Chorrillos and at Punta Hermosa and Punta Rocas. If you head instead to the beaches north or south of Lima, and you will find some of them untouched. Keep an eye out for opportunities to surf at **San Gallán,** one of Peru's few right point breaks in the Paracas National Reserve; **Pepinos** and **Cerro Azul,** near the mouth of the Cañete river valley; and **Playa Grande,** north of Lima, which is a challenging hollow point break for expert surfers. Good sources of surfing information include **Perú azul** (www.peruazul.com).

For surfing classes, call Rocio Larrañaga at **Surf School** (tel. 01/264-5100), who will pick you up at your hotel and lend you a wetsuit and board. Also recommended is Carlos Cabanillas at **Eternal Wave Peru** (tel. 9451-19998,

© LUIS GAMERO/PROMPERU

surfers off Lima's coast

www.eternalwaveperu.com), which has the Surfer's House for lodging. If you're just looking to rent, **Centro Comercial** (Caminos del Inca Tienda 158, Surco, tel. 01/372-5106) has both surfboards and skateboards. **Big Head** (Larcomar, Malecón de la Reserva 610, tel. 01/717-3145) sells new surfboards and body boards along with wetsuits. One of the better surf shops in Peru is **Focus** (Las Palmeras Block C, Playa Arica, Panamericana Sur Km 41, tel. 01/430-0444). The staff is knowledgeable about local surfing spots, rents boards at a good price, and even has a few hostel rooms.

TOUR AGENCIES AND GUIDES

Do not get hustled by agency reps at Lima's airport or bus stations. They will arrange travel packages that tend to be as expensive, or more expensive, than doing it on your own.

Sightseeing Agencies

A favorite travel agency in Lima is **Fertur Peru** (www.fertur-travel.com, 9am-7pm Mon.-Fri., 9am-1pm Sat.), run by the enterprising Siduith Ferrer, with offices in central Lima at the Plaza Mayor (Junín 211, tel. 01/427-2626) and Miraflores (Schell 485, tel. 01/242-1900). Fertur can buy a variety of bus and plane tickets for you and set up tours around Lima and trips to all of Peru's other attractions, including Cusco, Machu Picchu, and the Nasca Lines.

Peru's most reputable agency, in business for decades, is **Lima Tours** (Jirón de la Unión 1040, tel. 01/619-6900, www.limatours.com.pe), with offices in central Lima. Its city tours provide access to some of Lima's colonial mansions, including the pristine 17th-century mansion Casa de Aliaga. Because the company works with large international groups, it is best to make contact before arriving in Lima.

Run by an American-Peruvian couple, **Magical Cuzco Tours** (tel. 866/411-4622, www.magicalcuzcotours.com) offers several expeditions in Lima, including a half-day culinary tour and full-day visit to the nearby Caral and Pachacámac ruins. It can also help organize specialty tours to other parts of Peru.

Condor Travel (Armando Blondet 249, San

Isidro, tel. 01/615-3000) offers a day tour of colonial and contemporary Lima, as well as visits to other attractions like the Nasca Lines and Machu Picchu. A good agency for booking flights and other logistics is **Nuevo Mundo** (28 de Julio 1120, tel. 01/626-9393), with its office in Miraflores. Another reputable agency in Miraflores is **Wagonlit Travel** (Ricardo Palma 355, tel. 01/610-1600, www.cwtvacaciones.com.pe). An option for day tours in Lima is **Peru Smile** (28 de Julio 399 Of. 203, Miraflores, tel. 01/243-2152, perusmile@yahoo.com), which is run by Jorge Fernández and has tours and prices similar to Lima Vision but without the large groups.

Many of the recommended agencies sell tours run by **Lima Vision** (Chiclayo 444, Miraflores, tel. 01/447-7710, www.limavision.com, 24 hours daily), the city's standard pool service, which offers three- to four-hour daily tours of Lima's center (US$30), Museo Larco (US$40), Pachacámac (US$40), and Museo de Oro (US$50). Whether you buy from Lima Vision or from an agency, the cost is the same. All of Peru's main agencies are based in Lima.

Specialized Agencies

For those who can't make it to Paracas, **Ecocruceros** (Arequipa 4960, tel. 01/226-8530, www.ecocruceros.com) offers half-day boat tours from the port of Callao to see sea lions at the Islas Palomino.

Accommodations

There's no shortage of places to stay in Lima, whether you're looking for a five-star luxury hotel overlooking the Pacific or a backpacker hostel close to the action. If you're in town on business, San Isidro's financial district offers several high-end choices. In Barranco, you'll be in Lima's artsy center with a bohemian vibe and walking distance to a good selection of restaurants, bars, and *peñas*. Staying in Lima's colonial center is convenient if you want to be close to many of the city's churches and museums and don't mind the noise. A short taxi ride from Lima's downtown is the neighborhood of Breña. But overall, the best option is Miraflores, where you'll be walking distance to excellent restaurants and entertainment, charming parks lined with artists selling their work, and the city's magnificent oceanfront boardwalk.

CENTRAL LIMA AND PUEBLO LIBRE
US$10-25

In downtown Lima, the ◖ **Hostal Roma** (Ica 326, tel. 01/427-7576, www.hostalroma.8m.com, US$18 s, US$27 d, with breakfast and private bath) is a charming place catering to backpackers. With high ceilings, wood floors, and 10 different types of breakfast, Roma stands out from the rest. Internet access, safes, and airport transfers are available. A small attached café serves espresso, beer, and cocktails. The 36 rooms fill up fast, so make reservations early.

A new budget place in downtown Lima is **1900 Backpacker's Hostel** (Garcilaso de la Vega 1588, tel. 01/424-3358, www.1900hostel.com, US$8-10 dorm, US$30 d). This hostel gets strong reviews for its French-inspired ambiance but mixed reviews for service. It's located in a beautifully renovated mansion that has modern amenities to go along with the marble floors and high ceilings. It is centrally located, which means that you'll be close to many of Lima's best museums and churches but you'll also have to deal with a lot of noise.

Another good budget option in downtown Lima is **Hostal España** (Azángaro 105, tel. 01/428-5546 or 01/427-9196, www.hotelespanaperu.com, US$7 dorm, US$20 s, US$22 d with private bath). This backpacker classic is a labyrinth of tight halls and patios, decorated with hanging ivy, marble busts, and reproductions of colonial paintings. The rooms are small and basic with clean, shared baths and hot water. Despite its location, the hostel manages to disconnect itself from the hustle and be a peaceful escape. With a charming upstairs restaurant and neighboring Internet café, this place fills up quickly; make reservations early.

In Breña, the friendly **Hostal Iquique** (Iquique 758, tel. 01/433-4724 or 01/423-3699, www.hostal-iquique-lima.com, US$14 s, US$23 d, with breakfast) is a longtime backpacker favorite with good service, a kitchen, a rooftop terrace, and hot water. Rooms with tiled floors are not too noisy, and some even have TVs. Private baths cost an additional US$6-7.

Pueblo Libre's artist-owned **Guest House Marfil** (Parque Ayacucho 126, tel. 01/628-3791, casamarfil@yahoo.com, US$9 s, US$16 d) is a converted house with splashes of color, lots of paintings on the walls, and three resident cats. The bohemian rooms are private, making this a great value, and the shared baths are clean with plenty of hot water. There is free wireless Internet access and a group kitchen. They also offer an airport pickup for US$14. Banks and supermarkets are nearby.

US$25-50

Sitting at the end of a quiet park near the Museo de Arte is the recommended **Posada del Parque** (Parque Hernán Velarde 60, block 1, Petit Thouars, tel. 01/433-2412, www.incacountry.com, US$36 s, US$48 d). This hotel, in an old colonial house filled with traditional art, is the perfect escape from central Lima. The Parque de la Exposición, just blocks away, makes for great strolling. Monica, the attentive owner, provides two Internet-ready computers, firm beds, great "what to do" advice, and a sitting room with a TV and a DVD player.

Hostal Bonbini (Cailloma 209, tel. 01/427-6477, http://bonbini.tripod.com.pe, US$30 s, US$40 d, with breakfast) has large rooms with nice but dated furniture, cable TV, and big baths. Avoid noisy rooms on the street front. **Hotel Kamana** (Camaná 547, tel. 01/426-7204, www.hotelkamana.com, starting at US$40 s, US$48 d with breakfast) offers comfortable rooms with cable TV, Wi-Fi, safes, and private baths. There is a 24-hour snack bar, and the back rooms are quiet. This is a safe and reliable option for a good night's sleep.

US$50-100

Declared a historical monument in 1972, the **Gran Hotel Bolívar** (Jirón de la Unión 958, tel. 01/619-7171, www.granhotelbolivar.com. pe, US$75 s, US$80 d, with breakfast) is an attraction in itself. Walking into the employee-owned Hotel Bolívar is like going back to the 1920s, when it was built at the orders of President Augusto Leguía. As Lima's first luxury hotel, it housed visiting kings, dignitaries, and writers. Notable guests have included Charles de Gaulle, William Faulkner, Ernest Hemingway, and Mick Jagger. Today, the hotel plays an important role in Peruvian politics, serving as a favorite spot for politicians to give election-day speeches from its balconies to onlookers gathering in the Plaza San Martín. As a hotel, there are now better, less noisy options in Lima. Even if you don't spend the night, stop by for a pisco sour, which many Limeños say is one of the city's best.

Over US$150

The only five-star hotel in central Lima is the **Hotel Sheraton** (Paseo de la República 170, tel. 01/315-5000, www.sheraton.com.pe, US$170 s, US$180 d), a square tower that rises at the entrance to old town. This business hotel has a huge open atrium rising 19 floors. The normal rooms have older furniture and feel fourstarish. If you stay here, upgrade to the tower rooms on the upper floors, which have easy chairs, California king beds, elegant wood floors and paneling, and astounding views over Lima. Other amenities include a whirlpool tub, a sauna, and a gym. Beside the hotel is the **Plaza Real** shopping mall, which has a **Starbucks.**

SAN ISIDRO
US$10-25

The bulk of San Isidro's hotels are oriented

© CARLOS IBARRA/PROMPERU

the historical Gran Hotel Bolívar

toward high-class business travelers, but there is one great exception to this rule. **Youth Hostal Malka** (Los Lirios 165, San Isidro, tel. 01/442-0162, www.youthhostelperu.com, US$8 dorm, US$25 d) is a rare find and has its own rock-climbing wall. This converted home has simple clean rooms, Internet access, laundry service, and a grassy yard with a table-tennis table. The hostel is a block from a park, and a supermarket and a few restaurants are down the street. Rooms with private baths are US$5 more.

US$100-150

Like its sister hotels around the country, **Hotel Libertador San Isidro Golf** (Los Eucaliptos 550, San Isidro, tel. 01/518-6300, U.S. tel. 877/778-2281, www.libertador.com.pe, from US$150 s or d, with breakfast) is an elegant, classy act. These four-star rooms are a great value, with dark-stained furniture, elegant carpets, golf-course views, and all the creature comforts, including luxurious baths with tubs. There is an elegant pub downstairs with lots of wood, and the Ostrich House Restaurant serves

up ostrich and other delicious steaks. Features include a sauna, a whirlpool tub, and a gym. Like many higher-end hotels in Lima, rooms are cheaper on weekends.

Over US$150

At the top of El Olívar, a park shaded by ancient olive trees, **Sonesta Hotel El Olivar** (Pancho Fierro 194, San Isidro, tel. 01/712-6000, www.sonesta.com, US$153 s, US$164 d, with breakfast) has spacious though quite ordinary rooms, a beautiful sitting area with a bar, and a rooftop pool. Ask for a room with views over the olive grove.

Built in 1927, the **Country Club Lima Hotel** (Los Eucaliptos 590, San Isidro, tel. 01/611-9000, www.hotelcountry.com, US$289 s, US$309 d) has a classic turn-of-the-20th-century elegance. Couches fill a marble lobby decorated with Oriental rugs, dark wood, and high windows. Perks include an elegant restaurant, an English bar, a gym, and an outdoor pool. Suites are decorated with museum pieces from Museo de Osma. Ask for a room with a balcony or a view over the golf course, which, as a guest, you'll be able to play on.

Sandwiched between the Camino Real Mall and a glassy office park, **Swissôtel** (Via Central 150, San Isidro, tel. 01/421-4400, U.S. tel. 800/637-9477, www.swissotel-lima.com, US$299 s or d, with breakfast) is one of Peru's leading business hotels. All rooms have king beds, down comforters, large baths with tubs, and wireless Internet. Each floor has its own security card. You have your choice of food: Swiss, Italian, or Peruvian. An elegant swimming pool surrounded by a grassy lawn, a tennis court, a whirlpool tub, a sauna, and a gym make for a relaxing afternoon.

Los Delfines (Los Eucaliptos 555, tel. 01/215-7000, www.losdelfineshotel.com, US$200 s or d, buffet breakfast included) was an extravagant concept from the go-go Fujimori years, with the idea of having a pool full of leaping dolphins. The dolphins have since been relocated, but the hotel has comfortable rooms decked out with deep blue carpets and elegant tables and baths. Amenities include a casino, a luxurious outdoor pool, a spa with massages, an aerobics room, a sauna, and a whirlpool tub, and the restaurant serves first-class Mediterranean food.

Located in the heart of San Isidro's financial district, the **Westin Libertador** (Las Begonias 450, tel. 01/201-5000, www.libertador.com.pe, US$300 s or d, with breakfast) is the newest luxury hotel in Lima. This massive 301-room skyscraper includes two restaurants, a bar-lounge, a luxury spa, a heated indoor swimming pool, and Lima's top conference facility, which has hosted events by leading groups like the World Economic Forum.

Long-Term Stays

With a minimum stay of 15 days, **Loft** (Jorge Basadre 255, Of. 202, tel. 01/222-8983, www.loftapar.com), an apartment rental agency, offers travelers well-located, fully equipped apartments in San Isidro and Miraflores. Rates start at US$1,200 per month for a one-bedroom apartment. Two- and three-bedroom apartments are also available.

MIRAFLORES

Along with San Isidro, Miraflores is one of Lima's upscale districts. The shopping and restaurants are top-notch, and you're only a five-minute cab ride to nightlife action in Barranco.

US$10-25

A great place for budget travelers is **Explorer's House** (Alfredo León 158, tel. 01/241-5002, explorers_house@yahoo.es, US$8 dorm, US$12 s or d, with breakfast). The house-cum-hostel has a common kitchen and a TV room with a video library. The communal baths are clean, and laundry is US$1 per kilogram. The friendly owners, María Jesús and Víctor, give guests a remembrance gift on departure!

Casa del Mochilero (Cesareo Chacaltana 130A, 2nd Fl., tel. 01/444-9089, juan_kalua@hotmail.com, US$5 pp dorm with shared bath, US$14 s) is a clean and plain backpackers' hangout, about 10 minutes' walk from Parque Kennedy, with bunk rooms, shared baths, and a group kitchen.

Loki Inkahouse (José Galvez 576, tel. 01/651-2966 www.lokihostel.com, US$12 dorm, US$36 s or d, with breakfast), which used to be located right on Parque Kennedy, has moved a few blocks over but still has what backpackers want: clean rooms, Wi-Fi, and a restaurant and bar where fellow travelers can meet and socialize. It also has a women-only dorm room.

In Loki's old location on Parque Kennedy is **Pariwana Hostel** (Larco 189, tel. 01/242-4350, www.pariwana-hostel.com, US$10 dorm, US$36 d). This party hostel is located next to some of the city's busiest restaurants and bars. But if you don't feel like going far, the hostel has its own bar, pool table, table tennis, and a nice rooftop terrace.

It doesn't get more secure than at **Hitchhikers** (Bolognesi 400, tel. 01/242-3008, www.hhikersperu.com, US$11 dorm, US$26 s, US$28 d, with breakfast), an old house tucked away behind fortresslike walls. There's no scrimping on space here: Shared rooms have tall ceilings, the communal kitchen has two rooms, and there's even a huge parking area that doubles as a table-tennis arena.

The cheerful **Flying Dog Hostels** (Diez Canseco 117, tel. 01/242-7145; Lima 457, tel. 01/444-5753; Martir Olaya 280, tel. 01/447-0673, www.flyingdogperu.com, US$12 dorm, US$29 d, with breakfast) have become an institution in central Miraflores, and there are locations in other parts of Peru as well. The three Lima locations are all within a stone's throw of Parque Kennedy, and all guests eat breakfast at outdoor cafés on the park. The layout of each hostel is more or less the same: tight dormitory rooms, a few private rooms, sitting areas, clean baths, and lots of hot water. If you make a reservation, be sure you know for which Flying Dog venue you've made it. They also have options for longer stays.

Hostelling International (Casmiro Ulloa 328, tel. 01/446-5488, www.limahostell.com. pe, US$14 dorm, US$142 s) has a variety of rooms spread out in an old home with a sunny courtyard that is a 10-minute walk to Parque Kennedy. There is a travel agency in the lobby.

US$25-50

The charming **Hostal El Patio** (Diez Canseco 341, tel. 01/444-2107, www.hostalelpatio.net, US$45 s, US$56 d, with breakfast) is a memorable colonial home overflowing with plants and flowers and cheerfully painted walls. Large rooms have either tiled floors or carpet as well as homey furnishings and large windows. Ask for a mini suite for an additional US$5—you'll get your money's worth with a kitchenette. Rooms are interspersed with terraces, which are great places for reading or sunbathing.

US$50-100

A highly recommended place to stay while in Lima is the charming **Hotel Antigua Miraflores** (Grau 350, tel. 01/241-6166, www.peru-hotels-inns.com, US$92 s, US$106 d, with breakfast). This turn-of-the-20th-century mansion has all the comforts of a fine hotel and the warmth of a bed-and-breakfast. The rooms are large, cozy, and handsomely decorated with hand-carved furniture, local art,

and warm colors. Plus the remodeled baths have big tubs. There are plush couches in the downstairs sitting room, and six types of breakfast are served in a sunny black-and-white-tiled café. Suites are also available, with kitchens and whirlpool tubs.

Across the street from the handicrafts-haven Inka Market, the upscale **Casa Andina Centro** (Petit Thouars 5444, tel. 01/213-9739, www.casa-andina.com, US$72 s, US$80 d, with breakfast) puts you in the middle of the action, but without the hustle. Rooms have everything for comfort: modern baths, firm beds, down comforters, cable TV, mini fridges, air-conditioning, and Internet access in the lobby. The hotel chain has a second location slightly away from the center, **Casa Andina San Antonio** (Av. 28 de Julio 1088, tel. 01/213-9739, US$72 s, US$80 d, with breakfast), which is near some of Miraflores's best cafés, along with two other hotels, including a five-star version, nearby as well.

The **El Faro Inn** (Francia 857, tel. 01/242-0339, www.elfaroinn.com, US$44 s, US$60 d, with breakfast) is a modern hotel one block from the oceanfront. The small rooms are carpeted and have cable TV and basic furnishings. Other amenities include cheap Internet access, laundry, and a rooftop terrace. Also one block from the oceanfront is **Hostal Torre Blanca** (José Pardo 1453, tel. 01/447-0142, www.torreblancaperu.com, US$70 s or d, with breakfast), which offers large carpeted rooms with cable TV and mini fridges. There is free Internet access, laundry service, and airport transfers.

US$100-150

Aparthotel San Martín (San Martín 598, tel. 01/242-0500, www.sanmartinhotel.com, US$120 s, US$140 d) offers spacious suites with living rooms, double bedrooms, closets, baths, kitchens, cable TV, and phones. There are beds for two people and a pullout couch for two more. Floors 8-10 have wireless Internet access.

Over US$150

Most of the five-star hotels are in San Isidro, but there are a few gems in Miraflores, including the **Miraflores Park Hotel** (Malecón de la Reserva 1035, tel. 01/610-4000, www. mira-park.com, from US$290 s or d). This elegant glass high-rise, located on an old park overlooking the ocean, offers the best in service, comfort, and views in Lima. The grand marble entry is decorated with antique furnishings that are complemented by modern art. The luxurious rooms offer ocean views, elegant furnishings, cable TV with DVD players, fax machines, and wireless Internet. Other amenities include a video library, massages (US$90), a swimming pool, and a squash court.

The oceanfront **JW Marriott** (Malecón de la Reserva 615, tel. 01/217-7000, www. marriotthotels.com, US$157 s or d) occupies prime real estate overlooking the Pacific Ocean and just across the street from the deluxe full-service Larcomar mall. The rooms live up to five-star Marriott quality and are nearly silent despite the busy street below. For the best view, ask for a room on one of the upper floors with an ocean view. Perks include glass-enclosed bars and restaurants, a casino, a pool, and a tennis court. A Starbucks is on the ground floor.

One of the newest high-end hotels in Lima is the **Hilton Lima Miraflores** (La Paz 1099, tel. 01/200-8000, www.hilton.com, from US$149 s or d). The Hilton mixes colonial decorations with modern fixtures. The hotel's 207 rooms all include unique lattice woodwork, Wi-Fi, and 37-inch TVs. Other amenities include a heated rooftop swimming pool, a fitness center, and a restaurant with a street-level patio.

BARRANCO
US$10-25
The Point (Malecón Junín 300, tel. 01/247-7997, www.thepointhostels.com, US$10-12 dorm, US$25 s or d, with breakfast) is a backpacker option with everything a traveler needs: Wi-Fi, long-distance calling, a sitting room with cable TV, nice bunk beds with shared baths, cheap lunches, a pool table, surfing lessons, a book exchange, a travel agency, a grassy lawn, and an outdoor bar. This 11-room restored 19th-century house is just paces away from Barranco's best bars and sweeping ocean views. There are frequent barbecues and nightly outings to nearby bars, which give guests a discount.

Backpackers Inn (Malecón Castilla 260, tel. 01/247-3709, backpackersinnperu@hotmail. com, US$10 dorm, US$35 d with breakfast) is another option that's less hectic and more quiet. Some rooms open onto the oceanfront, and a nearby path leads down to the beach. The inn has a communal kitchen, a sofa lounge, a dining room with board games, a TV and a DVD player, Wi-Fi, and plenty of visitor information.

Aquisito (Centenario 114, tel. 01/247-0712, US$18 s, U$29 d) is a great bed-and-breakfast. The place is small and cozy, located on a noisy part of Barranco but incredibly quite inside. Rooms are comfortable, and staff are quite friendly and helpful.

US$25-50
D'Osma Bed & Breakfast (Pedro de Osma 240, tel. 01/251-4178, www.deosma.com, US$30-44 s, US$50 d, with breakfast) is a great option if you are looking for a tranquil, family-oriented environment.

US$50-100
3B Barranco's Bed & Breakfast (Centenario 130, tel. 01/247-6915, www.3bhostal.com, US$77 s, US$88 d) is the newest addition to a group of comfy and well-equipped hostels and bed-and-breakfasts in Barranco. With a neat, minimalistic design and decor, the rooms are clean, bright, and spacious, with very comfy beds and impeccable baths. The hostel is on a very busy street but two blocks away from the ocean and a few more from all of Barranco's nightlife. It offers Wi-Fi and laundry.

US$100-150
Second Home Peru (Domeyer 366, tel. 01/247-5522, www.secondhomeperu.com, US$115 s, US$130 d, with breakfast) is inside the home of Víctor Delfin, a prominent Peruvian painter and sculptor, and his works fill the first floor of the house as well as the five elegant guest rooms. Lilian Delfin, his daughter, is a

welcoming and helpful host who will lead you on a morning visit to Víctor's studio. A swim in the cool pool overlooking the ocean from a cliff, with a lion fountain spouting above, is a must. The high ceilings, crisp white linens, and designer baths make any visitor to Second Home feel simultaneously at ease and refined. All rooms have a cable Internet connection. A night in this hotel should not be missed.

Over US$150

Far and away the most exclusive option in Barranco, and far and away the most expensive, is the new **B Arts Boutique** (San Martín 301, tel. 01/206-0800, www.hotelb.pe, from US$450 s or d), a former presidential seaside retreat built in 1914. The ornate facade, Italian marble, and wood columns are accompanied by all of the modern amenities. Guest areas include a cozy library and a rooftop patio overlooking the Pacific. The hotel's restaurant has a menu that was prepared by Oscar Velarde, the owner of Lima's acclaimed La Gloria restaurant. Oh, and the hotel is also connected to the **Lucia de la Puente Art Gallery** (www.gluciadelapuente.com), which means that guests can enjoy private viewings. Even if you don't have the cash to spring for a night, if you like historical buildings, this could be worth a quick visit anyway.

Food

Peruvian cuisine has an extraordinary range of flavors and ingredients, and nowhere is that more evident than in Lima. The range of high-quality restaurants is extraordinary. The best lunch deal is always the fixed-price *menú,* which typically includes three well-prepared courses. Upscale restaurants tack on a 10 percent service charge and an 18 percent value-added tax.

The center has good budget eateries, including some of the best *chifa* (Chinese-Peruvian food) in town. San Isidro and Miraflores have the most interesting and refined restaurants, where dozens of Cordon Bleu-trained chefs busily cater to their refined Lima clientele.

CENTRAL LIMA AND PUEBLO LIBRE

Other than the cluster of restaurants around Pasaje Nicolás de Ribera El Viejo and Pasaje Santa Rosa, central Lima's dining options are spread out. That said, it is worth taking a cab to some of them, especially the classics in Pueblo Libre.

Cafés, Bakeries, and Ice Cream

Antigua Taberna Queirolo (San Martín 1090, tel. 01/460-0441, www.antiguatabernaqueirolo. com, 10am-10pm daily, US$8) is a charming Spanish-style café that has been open since 1880. This is a good place to come in the afternoon or evenings to sample pisco (fortified wine), made in the winery next door. Quierolo is famous for its *chilcano,* a mix of pisco and ginger ale with a touch of lime juice. Customers normally order a bottle of pisco and a liter of ginger ale, and then mix their own drinks. This is an excellent way to pass a few hours with friends. There is a slim but good menu that includes salted ham sandwiches, tamales, and *papa relleno* (stuffed potatoes).

Opening onto the lawns of the Museo Larco is the tasteful **Café del Museo** (Bolívar 1515, tel. 01/462-4757, www.museolarco.org, 9am-10pm daily, US$15). Pablo Lazarte leads the small kitchen and sends out delicious plates of tender lamb, steamed sea bass, and shrimp *causa.*

Across the street from the presidential palace is historic **El Cordano** (Ancash 202, tel. 01/427-0181, 8am-8pm daily, US$10), a century-old establishment that was a favored haunt of writers and intellectuals. Though its facade is a bit tattered, this is an excellent place to come for a pisco sour and one of its famous ham sandwiches.

Peruvian

If you are staying in Pueblo Libre or visiting the Museo Larco, eat lunch in the neighborhood. **El Bolivariano** (Pasaje Santa Rosa 291, tel. 01/261-9565, www.elbolivariano.com, 10am-10pm daily, US$12) is a time-honored Lima restaurant in an elegant republican-style home that is visited mainly by Peruvians. The menu includes Peruvian classics such as *seco de cabrito* (stewed goat), *arroz con pato* (rice with duck), and *anticuchos* (marinated beef heart served on a skewer). A buffet is offered on Sunday, which is a good opportunity to sample several Peruvian dishes. On Friday and Saturday night, the restaurant turns into a popular bar, where locals dance between tables while sipping pisco.

OK, it is a chain, but **Pardo's** (Pasaje Santa Rosa 153, tel. 01/427-8123, www.pardoschicken.com.pe, noon-11pm daily, US$10) still serves the best spit-roasted chicken, with affordable lunch menus and open-air tables right off the Plaza Mayor. It also serves *anticuchos,* brochettes, and *chicharrones.*

In the same pedestrian walkway, **T'anta** (Pasaje Nicolás de Rivera el Viejo 142-148, tel. 01/428-3115, 9am-10pm Mon.-Sat., 9am-6pm Sun., US$7-14), a Gaston Acurio restaurant, serves up refined plates of Peruvian favorites *lomo saltado* and *recoto relleno* as well as creative new inventions like *ají de gallina* ravioli.

A more upscale spot is **Los Virtrales de Gemma** (Ucayali 332, tel. 01/426-7796, 8am-5pm Mon.-Sat., US$10), in a restored colonial home one block from the Plaza Mayor. The hardworking owners have created an excellent and varied menu of Peruvian and international food.

Though a bit faded from its past glory, **L'Eau Vive** (Ucayali 370, tel. 01/427-5612, 12:30pm-3pm and 7:30pm-9:30pm Mon.-Sat., US$7) still serves up wholesome and delicious lunch *menús* prepared by a French order of nuns. Dinners feature cocktails, the singing of "Ave María," and an eclectic selection of international entrées.

In Breña, **La Choza Náutica** (Breña 204, off 1st block of Arica, tel. 01/423-8087, www. chozanautica.com, 10am-10pm daily, US$9-11) is a former hole-in-the-wall *cebichería* that has become more upscale and successful over the years. It serves special ceviches (including an "erotic" version) and *tiraditos* in huge portions. The restaurant has three other locations in Lima.

Ceviche

Patrons of **Chez Wong** (Enrique León García 114, La Victoria, tel. 01/470-6217, noon-5pm Mon.-Sat., US$25) won't find a sign advertising the restaurant outside. But diners flock to this restaurant for one thing and one thing only: arguably one of the best ceviches in Lima, if not all of Peru. The restaurant is literally the home of iconoclastic chef Javier Wong, considered by many to be a culinary master. While several of Peru's top chefs have expanded to the United States and Europe, Wong has maintained a loyal cultlike following at his small no-frills restaurant, where he prepares ceviche in front of his guests. No menus are available, so if you're looking for anything other than ceviche, this won't be the place for you. Also, be sure to call ahead, as reservations are a must.

Chifa

The influence of Chinese immigration to Peru is perhaps most evident in the popularity of Chinese-Peruvian cuisine, known as *chifa*. When in central Lima, do not miss the opportunity to sample chifa at one of the largest Chinatowns in South America. There are at least a dozen places spread along the town's two main streets, Capón and Paruro. The best known in Lima's Chinatown is **Wa Lok** (Paruro 878, tel. 01/427-2750, 9am-11pm Mon.-Sat., 9am-10pm Sun., US$12-17), serving more than 20 types of dim sum. Try *ja kao dim sum,* a mixture of pork and shrimp with rice, or *siu mai de chanco,* shredded pork with mushroom and egg pasta. A good, less expensive alternative to Wa Lok, with a more elegant dining room, is **Salon Capon** (Paruro 819, tel. 01/426-9286, 9am-10pm daily, US$8-10), serving peking duck, *langostinos Szechuan* (sautéed shrimps with *ají* pepper), and *chuleta kin tou* (grilled sweet pork). Both have lovely display cases of after-lunch desserts.

SAN ISIDRO

San Isidro's restaurant and nightlife scene lives mostly on the Avenida de los Conquistadores, where you will find some of Lima's newest and most upscale restaurants.

Cafés, Bakeries, and Ice Cream

For those who want a good place to read, **La Baguette** (Aliaga 456, tel. 01/715-5690, 7am-midnight daily, US$7) has a nice second-story balcony and a long list of sandwiches on real baguettes. A *chicharron,* a delicious pork sandwich with sweet potatoes and onion toppings, is recommended. **Don Mamino** (Conquistadores 790, tel. 01/719-7000, 7am-11pm daily) has gourmet desserts and fresh-baked breads. **The Ice Cream Factory** (Conquistadores 395, tel. 01/222-2633, 10am-9:30pm daily) has a good range of ice creams and affordable sandwiches. The geranium-lined patio of **La Bonbonneire** (Burgos 415, tel. 01/421-2447, 8am-11pm Tues.-Sat., 8am-9pm Sun., US$14-20) is straight out of France, as are the delicate sandwiches of cream cheese and smoked trout. The patio of **T'anta** (Pancho Fierro 117, tel. 01/421-9708, 10am-10pm Mon.-Sat., 10am-7pm Sun., US$7-14) is an excellent place to linger over a cup of coffee, a glass of wine, or a rich chocolate dessert. The very best ice cream in Peru is at **Cafeladeria 4D** (Las Begonias 580, 7am-11:30pm Mon.-Sat., 11am-9pm Sun.). *Lúcuma* and chocolate make an unbeatable double scoop. Down the road is **La Gran Fruta** (Las Begonias 463, tel. 01/422-0606, www.la-granfruta.com.pe, 8am-11pm Mon.-Fri., 8am-11:45pm Sat.-Sun.), which serves up delicious juices as well as fruit salads using *granadilla* and *chirimoya.* **Delicass** (Las Begonias 510, tel. 01/440-5050, www.delicass.com.pe, 7am-midnight daily) is a good lunch choice, with an excellent selection sandwiches and salads, and delicious desserts like *lúcuma* mousse.

Peruvian

Punta Sal (Conquistadores 948, tel.

01/441-7431, www.puntasal.com, 11am-5pm daily, US$10-14) is a large, casual place for good seafood and ceviche. The lunch-only **Segundo Muelle** (Conquistadores 490, tel. 01/717-9998, www.segundomuelle.com, noon-5pm daily, US$10-15) successfully combines pastas with seafood and tasty ceviche. Try the ravioli stuffed with crabmeat or lasagna with shrimp and artichoke.

San Isidro's classic Peruvian restaurant, with over 35 years in the business, is **José Antonio** (Bernardo Monteagudo 200, tel. 01/264-0188, www.joseantonio.com.pe, 12:30pm-4:30pm and 7:30pm-midnight daily, US$14-17). Said to have the best *lomo saltado* in town, the restaurant also offers *ají de gallina, cau cau,* and *causa* with *camarones.* Afterward, try *picarones,* a sweet colonial-era doughnut-like dessert.

International

With a culture of ceviche, it isn't surprising that Lima has latched on to sushi. **Osaka** (Conquistadores 999, tel. 01/222-0405, www.osaka.com.pe, 12:30pm-4pm and 7:30pm-1am daily, US$9-12) is doing with Japanese food what many Peruvian restaurants have done with international cuisine: fusion. *Camote* (sweet potato) tempura and Inca rolls are dinner highlights. One of the first to blend Japanese cuisine with Peruvian ingredients was **Matsuei** (Manuel Bañon 260, tel. 01/422-4323, 12:30pm-3:30pm and 7:30pm-11pm Mon.-Sat., US$15). Opened in the 1970s by a young Nobu Matsuhisa, now a world-famous chef, Matsuei is a cozy sushi bar with delicious maki and sashimi.

A really good pizza place is **La Linterna** (Libertadores 311, tel. 01/440-3636, 12:30pm-4pm and 6:30pm-11:30pm Mon.-Thurs., 12:30pm-4pm and 6:30am-12:30am Fri.-Sat., 12:30pm-4pm and 6:30pm-11pm Sun., US$10). Go for any of the thin-crust pizzas, or try *tallarines verdes* (spaghetti in spinach pesto), a Peruvian comfort food.

A casual place for great Mexican and margaritas is **Como Agua Para Chocolate** (Pancho Fierro 108, tel. 01/222-0297, noon-midnight Mon.-Sat., noon-10pm Sun., US$8), with brightly colored walls and friendly service. If you are in the mood for an Argentine grill, and an all-meat menu, head to **La Carreta** (Rivera Navarrete 740, tel. 01/442-2690, 11am-11pm daily, US$20-30).

Fine Dining

Featured in many local cookbooks, the recipes of **Malabar** (Camino Real 101, tel. 01/440-5200, www.malabar.com.pe, 12:30pm-3:30pm and 7:30pm-11:30pm daily, US$15-20) have garnered national and international acclaim. The flavors are a mix of the Mediterranean (chef Pedro Miguel Schiaffino studied in Italy), Amazonia (then he lived in Iquitos), and finally classic Peruvian. The intimate restaurant, with clean white tablecloths, is the perfect fusion for a traveler who's been all over the country.

To live classic Lima's elegance, you can do nothing better than have a pisco sour on the wide open patio of **Perroquet** (Los Eucaliptos 590, tel. 01/611-9000, www.hotelcountry.com, 11am-11pm daily, US$15-20), inside the Country Club Lima Hotel. Follow your sour with grilled *chita* (Peruvian grunt fish), and finally top it off with a medley of Peruvian fruit sorbets.

A local favorite is **El Kapallaq** (Reducto 1505, tel. 01/444-4149, noon-5pm daily, US$14-18), which is located in a two-story converted house and includes a chef's table in the kitchen. The owner, of Basque ancestry, throws in twists from his home country, dishing up favorites like *marmitako* (a seafood stew). But the Peruvian influence is just as strong, and classics like *arroz con conchas y langostinos* (rice with scallops and shrimp) and *chita* are also present. This classic restaurant is a lunch-only establishment.

MIRAFLORES

Even if you are on a limited budget, splurging on one of Miraflores's top restaurants will be a memorable experience you will not regret.

Cafés, Bakeries, and Ice Cream

One of Lima's classic cafés is surely **Haiti** (Diagonal 160, tel. 01/445-0539, 7am-2am Sun.-Thurs., 7am-3am Fri.-Sat., US$10), in operation for more than half a century on Parque Kennedy. Indoor and sidewalk tables are overflowing with Peruvians day and night. Haiti is less known for its food than its intellectual conversation, good coffee, and pisco sours. Right across the street is **La Tiendecita Blanca** (Larco 111, tel. 01/445-9797, 7am-midnight daily, US$14), an elegant Swiss-style café and deli that has been in business since 1937. Anything you eat here will be excellent.

For a quick sandwich on Parque Kennedy, go to **La Lucha** (Benavides 308, tel. 01/241-5953, www.lalucha.com.pe, 6am-1am Sun.-Thurs., 6am-3am Fri.-Sat., US$4). A recommended sandwich is the *chicharron* (fried pork with sweet potato). It has another location literally across the street on Pasaje Champagnat.

Try the *lomo saltado* sandwich at **Pasquale Hnos. Sangucheria** (Comandante Espinar 651, tel. 01/369-0012, 9am-midnight Mon.-Fri., 9am-1am Sat., 9am-11pm Sun., US$6). This sandwich joint makes fast food fancy and purely Peruvian, since all sandwiches are inspired by classic Peruvian plates.

San Antonio (Vasco Núñez de Balboa 762, tel. 01/626-1303, 7am-10:45pm daily) is a bakery, café, and deli with 36 gourmet sandwiches (including smoked salmon and Italian salami), huge salads with organic lettuce, and an extensive dessert case with an out-of-this-world *tortaleta de lúcuma*. Across the street, **T'anta** (28 de Julio 888, tel. 01/447-8377, 8am-midnight daily) is also good, but the menu is all Peruvian.

For dessert, Limeños will tell you that **Cafeladeria 4D** (Angamos Oeste 408, tel. 01/445-4228, 7am-11:45am Mon.-Thurs., 7am-12:30am Fri.-Sat., 7am-midnight Sun.) has the best ice cream and gelato in the city, and they may be right. But if you're wanting chocolate, head over to **Chocolates Helena** (Chiclayo 897, tel. 01/242-8899, www.chocolateshelena.com, 10:30am-7:30pm daily), where the *chocotejas* and truffles are hard to resist. **Manolo** (Larco 608, tel. 01/444-2244, 7:15am-1am Mon.-Thurs., 7:15am-2am Fri., 8:15am-2am Sat., 8:15am-1am Sun.) has an extensive dessert menu, but it is best known for its *churros*.

© RYAN DUBÉ

For a quick sandwich, try La Lucha.

Ceviche

You will not regret the cab ride to **Pescados Capitales** (La Mar 1337, tel. 01/421-8808, 12:30pm-5pm Tues.-Sun., US$15), a witty play on words (*pescados* means "fish" but rhymes with *pecados,* or "sins") that makes sense when you see the menu. Each dish is named for a virtue or a sin; Diligence will bring you a ceviche of tuna and *conchas negras,* while Patience will bring you a ceviche of shrimps with curry and mango chutney. At a more affordable price, but also highly recommended, is **Punto Azul** (San Martín 395, tel. 01/445-8078, 11am-4pm Sun.-Wed., 11am-4pm and 7pm-midnight Thurs.-Sat., US$10-12). In addition to ceviche, it serves other delicious dishes from the sea, like *arroz con mariscos* (rice with seafood). One plate is enough for two, but arrive early because after 1:30pm you'll have to wait to get a seat.

Ceviche is elegantly served in martini glasses at Gaston Acurio's **La Mar Cebichería** (La Mar 770, tel. 01/421-3365, 11am-5pm daily, US$15-20). No reservations are accepted and lines can get long, so plan for a leisurely lunch over

several types of ceviche, cold beer, grilled fish, and crisp white wine.

Peruvian

Long overshadowed by dishes from the coast and the Andes, Amazonian cuisine is just starting to make headway into Lima's restaurant scene. At the forefront of this movement is **Amaz** (La Paz 1079, tel. 01/221-9393, 12:30pm-11:30pm Mon.-Thurs., 12:30pm-midnight Fri.-Sat., 12:30pm-4:30pm Sun., US$30), where Malabar's Pedro Miguel Schiaffino serves up a variety of flavors and plates inspired by the Peruvian rainforest. The menu includes Amazonian staples like *tacacho con cecina* (roasted green plantains with dried pork), smoked *paiche,* and more exotic options likes *churros pishpirones* (giant Amazonian snails).

If you're looking for something a little closer to home, **Cesar** (La Mar 814, tel. 01/221-6955, noon-5:30pm daily, US$12-15), formerly known as Mi Causa, is an excellent restaurant. It serves delicious plates of the classic Peruvian comfort food, the creamy potato-based *causa*. There are the classic tuna and avocado offerings, but why not try a *lomo saltado* or *cauchi de camarones* (crayfish stew) *causa?*

Budget eaters flock to **Rincón Chami** (Esperanza 154, tel. 01/444-4511, 9am-9pm Mon.-Sat., 9am-5pm Sun., US$7) for ceviche, tamales, *brochetas,* and *lomo saltados,* dished up in a diner-like atmosphere. Each day there is a different special of the house.

Pampa de Amancaes (Armendariz 546, tel. 01/445-5099, www.pampadeamancaes.com, 12:30pm-4pm and 6pm-11pm daily, US$15) has an excellent menu that offers classics like ceviche, the creamy *ají de gallina,* and *lomo saltado.* Drinks can include a pisco sour. For dessert try the *suspiro de Limeña* (Spanish for "the *Limeña*'s sigh") or the *mazamorra morada* (a pudding-like dish made from purple corn).

For a buffet of comida criolla, try **Brujas de Cachiche** (Bolognesi 472, tel. 01/447-1133, www.brujasdecachiche.com.pe, noon-midnight Mon.-Sat., noon-4pm Sun., US$25-40). The buffet (Tues.-Sun.) includes a tour de force of centuries of indigenous Peruvian cooking. **El Señorio de Sulco** (Malecón Cisneros 1470, tel. 01/441-0183, www.senoriodesulco.com, 12:30pm-11pm Mon.-Sat., 12:30pm-4pm Sun., US$25) also has an extravagant daily lunch buffet and a range of seafood plates. Try the *chupe de camarones,* a cream-based soup full of ocean shrimp, yellow potatoes, and *ají* pepper.

International

La Trattoria di Mambrino (Manuel Bonilla 106, tel. 01/446-7002, 1pm-4pm and 7pm-11:30pm Mon.-Wed., 1pm-4pm and 7pm-12:30am Thurs.-Sat., 1pm-4pm and 7pm-midnight Sun., US$12) is owned by a Roman and may be Peru's best Italian restaurant. This cozy place serves authentic Italian dishes like gnocchi with pesto genovese, risotto with wild mushrooms, pan-fried shrimp with wine sauce, and porcini mushroom pizza. Another good Italian option is Mambrino's sister restaurant, **La Bodega de la Trattoria** (General Borgoño 784, tel. 01/241-6899, noon-midnight-daily, US$12).

Lima doesn't have many Indian restaurants, but thankfully there is **Mantra** (Benavides 1761, tel. 01/445-0127, www.mantraperu.com, 12:30pm-11pm Mon.-Thurs., 12:30-midnight Fri.-Sat., 12:30pm-5pm Sun., US$10). Indian-born chef and owner Jay Patel offers delicious Indian dishes. Try the chicken madras with garlic naan bread and a chai tea.

Located at Larcomar mall, **Makoto** (Malecón de la Reserva 610, tel. 01/444-5030, www.makotosushibar.com, 12:30pm-midnight Mon.-Thurs., 12:30pm-1am Fri.-Sat., 12:30pm-11pm Sun., US$20) is an excellent, though touristy, sushi restaurant with high prices. **Edo Sushi Bar** (Berlin 601, tel. 01/434-4545, www.edosushibar.com, 12:30pm-3:30pm and 7pm-11pm Mon.-Sat., 1pm-4pm Sun., US$15) is a cool, quiet restaurant for authentic sushi located a few doors down from the Canadian embassy.

Fine Dining

No restaurant has done more to put Peruvian cuisine on the map than **Astrid y Gastón Casa Moreyra** (Av. Paz Soldán 290, Casa Hacienda Moreyra, San Isidro, tel. 01/242-5387, www.astridygaston.com, 12:30pm-3pm and 7pm-11pm Mon.-Sat., US$35-40). This restaurant has inspired a generation of chefs by instilling pride in local ingredients and dishes while promoting creativity in the kitchen. While no longer the new kid on the block, Astrid y Gastón is still one of the best Peruvian restaurants. Indeed, in 2013 it was named the best restaurant in Latin America by the UK-based William Reed Business Media. In early 2014, the restaurant moved from its original location in Miraflores to Casa Hacienda Moreyra, a refurbished colonial hacienda in San Isidro.

This adventurous gourmet restaurant is the labor of love of a Peruvian-German couple, Gastón Acurio and his wife, Astrid Gutsche, who met at the Cordon Bleu in Paris. Start your evening with creative pisco drinks such as the *aguaymanto* sour, made with pisco puro and the tangy juice of *aguaymanto* fruit. For a starter, try the peking guinea pig, described as a guinea pig "disguised" as a peking duck.

Then move on to never-before-sampled entrées such as kid goat basted in algaroba honey and marinated in *chicha de jora,* or river prawns served with red curry, coconut milk, and jasmine rice. Save room, as the desserts are the best part: toasted chocolate croutons with white peaches in vanilla syrup and Peruvian ice cream. There are plans to move the restaurant to San Isidro, so check the website or call to confirm the address.

Nipping at the heels of Astrid y Gastón's for best Peruvian restaurant is Virgilio Martínez's **Central** (Santa Isabel 376, 01/242-8515, www.centralrestaurante.com.pe, 1:30pm-3:30pm and 8pm-11:30pm Mon.-Wed., 1:30pm-3:30pm and 8pm-midnight Thurs.-Fri., 8pm-midnight Sat., US$30-40). Martínez's restaurant in London, called **Lima,** was awarded a Michelin star in 2013, the first Peruvian restaurant to get the award. A former executive chef at Astrid y Gastón, Martínez is known for traveling the country's high Andes and swampy Amazon rainforest in search of little-known ingredients, which he uses to garnish dishes like farm raised *arapaima,* one of the largest fresh water fish in the world, and roasted grouper. Top it off with a coca leaf sour.

Another top contender is **Rafael** (San Martín 300, tel. 01/242-4149, www.rafaelosterling.com, 1pm-3:30pm and 8pm-midnight Mon.-Fri., 8pm-midnight Sat., US$30), the creation of Rafael Osterling, who left behind law school to take up his true passion: cooking. Located in a turn-of-the-century house, Rafael cites his mother's home-cooked meals and his globe-trotting as inspirations for his fusion of Peruvian and international dishes. Try the *arroz con pato,* rice with duck slowly cooked in dark beer and onion relish, or the *ají de camarones,* a river shrimp stew. Osterling's other top-rated restaurant is the relatively new **El Mercado** (Hipolito Unanue 203, tel. 01/221-1322, noon-5pm Tues.-Sun., US$30), a great place for ceviche.

The elegant **Huaca Pucllana** (General Borgoño block 8, tel. 01/445-4042, www.resthuacapucllana.com, noon-4pm and 7pm-midnight daily, US$25) has a magical feel when the ruins of the same name, only six meters away, are lit up at night. Guests sit at linen-covered tables on an open-air patio next to the ruins and enjoy dishes such as grilled portobello mushroom salad with goat cheese, rabbit stewed in red wine, mushroom sauce over polenta, and grilled lamb chops.

If you're in the mood for Mediterranean, head to **La Gloria** (Atahualpa 201, tel. 01/445-5705, www.lagloriarestaurant.com, 1pm-4pm and 8pm-midnight Mon.-Sat., US$30). Especially good are the *carpaccio de pescado* with ginger and the seared tuna steaks.

Lima's time-honored seaside gourmet restaurant, Rosa Naútica, is a bit faded. But a good competitor, **Costanera 700** (El Ejército 421, tel. 01/421-7508, noon-5pm and 7pm-11pm Mon.-Sat., noon-5pm Sun., US$30), is recognized as one of the better restaurants in Lima. This is a good place to come for an elegant array of both Peruvian and international cuisine.

Chifa

Central Lima's time-honored *chifa* restaurant **Wa Lok** (Angamos Oeste 700, tel. 01/447-1314, noon-11pm daily, US$15-20) also has a Miraflores location. You'll have to ignore the charmless first-floor casino before you can settle down into your fish with corn sauce or steaming stir-fry.

Vegetarian

When you walk through a health food store to get to the restaurant, you know lunch will be balanced and nutritious. **Madre Natura** (Chiclayo 815, tel. 01/445-2522, 8am-9pm Mon.-Sat., US$6) is all that and is well-priced. Sit down for a soy-based hamburger, and leave with wheat bread in hand.

Markets

Plaza Vea (Arequipa 4651, 8am-10pm daily), **Metro** (Schell 250, 24 hours daily), **Wong** (Bajada Balta 626, 8am-11pm daily), and the upscale **Vivanda** (Benavides 495, 24 hours) have large selections of international and domestic foods.

© RYAN DUBÉ

Tostaduria Bisetti

BARRANCO AND THE SOUTH

Slow-paced Barranco has a number of romantic eateries and cafés, and on the weekend, outdoor food stalls fill a walkway near the central plaza.

Cafés, Bakeries, and Ice Cream

Tostaduria Bisetti (Pedro de Osma 116, tel. 01/713-9566, 8am-11pm daily) is the best café in Barranco. Not only does it serve outstanding locally sourced organic coffee, the best we've tried in Lima, but it also roasts its beans in-house and has a "coffee laboratory" in the back. Its comfortable sofas, black-and-white photos on the walls, and hardwood floors make it a great place to sit back and relax. If you're lucky, there may be live music when you arrive. The café is located right cross from Barranco's main plaza.

Sofa Café (San Martín 480, tel. 01/719-4384, 8:15am-midnight Sun.-Thurs., 8:15am-1am Fri.-Sat.) is farther away from Barranco's plaza but offers a good menu that includes specialty coffees, cold Peruvian drinks like *chicha morada,* and sandwiches and desserts like sweet waffles and tiramisu mousse. Another good option if you want to relax for a bit is to grab a coffee at the open-air patio of **Dédalo,** the artisanal shop.

Ceviche

CantaRana (Génova 101, tel. 01/247-7274, 11am-5pm Sun.-Mon., 11am-11pm Tues.-Sat., US$8-11), a no-frills lunch place with loads of history, serves up great *cebiche* and a range of seafood. The unassuming **Costa Sur** (Chorrillos 180, tel. 01/252-0150, noon-4pm Tues.-Sun., US$8-10), in Chorrillos, has fried shrimp and *conchas a la parmesana* worth a taxi ride.

Peruvian

With bow tie-clad waiters and an old piano, **Las Mesitas** (Grau 341, tel. 01/477-4199, noon-11pm daily, US$5-7) has an old-timey feel. For those on a budget, this is a great place to sample Peruvian food, including *humitas,* tamales, *sopa criolla, ocopa arequipeña,* and *lomo saltado.*

Lunch buffets are popular in Lima, and Barranco seems to have an especially high per capita number of restaurants serving up just that. In order of preference, we recommend **Puro Perú** (República de Panamá 258, tel. 01/477-0111, 12:30pm-5pm daily, US$15) and the ocean-side **Rustica** (Playa Barranco, tel. 01/717-8365, 12:30pm-midnight daily, US$15). There is also a **Rustica** on Barranco's plaza.

Mi Perú (Av. Lima 861, Plaza Butters, tel. 01/408-2431, noon-5:30pm Tues.-Sun., US$8-10) is what you call in Peru a *huarique,* a hole-in-the-wall with good food. In this case it's all about the *concentrado de cangrejo* (crab soup), the best you will find in the country. *Cebiches* are good here, too, but go for the soup; it's worth every penny. Another *huarique* that is popular among locals is **Café Tostado** (Nicolas de Pierola 232, tel. 01/247-7133, noon-9pm daily, US$15). Don't let the name fool you; this place isn't known for its coffee. Indeed, it doesn't even serve coffee, just delicious food on long wooden communal tables. It is known for its fried rabbit, which is marinated in orange sauce and served with sweet potato. Other dishes vary depending on the day and could include a beef stew or *tacu-tacu.*

For a steak and red wine fix, ■**Parrillados El Hornero** (Malecón Grau 983, tel. 01/251-8109, noon-midnight Mon.-Sat., noon-6pm Sun., US$8-10), in Chorrillos, is a must. The second-floor tables have impressive ocean views, and the grilled provolone and Argentine baby beef will do for your palate what it won't do for your cholesterol.

International

All right, you probably didn't come to Lima to eat hamburgers, but if you just need a burger fix, the best place in all of Lima is **Twist** (Grau 384, tel. 01/252-9228, www.twistgourmetburgers.com, noon-11pm Tues.-Sat., noon-5pm Sun., US$10). Your mouth-watering options include an Alpaca burger or a Barranco burger, which includes *anticucho* sauce and chili peppers.

Fine Dining

Compared to Miraflores or San Isidro, fine dining options are more limited in Barranco, but there are a few exceptions, like **Amor Amar** (Jirón García y García 175, tel. 01/615-9595, 12:30pm-4pm and 8pm-midnight Mon.-Sat., 12:30pm-5pm Sun., US$15-25). The restaurant has a good menu of seafood specialties, like *cebiches, tiraditos,* and grilled octopus. Other options include risottos, duck, lamb, and beef. Cocktails are well done, and the varied wine list is pretty impressive.

Pizza

The best pizzas are at **Antica Trattoria** (San Martín 201, tel. 01/247-3443, noon-midnight daily, US$10-15), a charming Italian eatery with stucco walls, exposed beams, and rustic furniture. The lasagna is excellent, as is the array of homemade pastas.

Markets

The large modern supermarket **Metro** (Grau 513, 9am-10:30pm daily) is within walking distance of all Barranco hotels.

Information and Services

VISITOR INFORMATION

Free maps and visitor information are available at **Iperú** (Jorge Chávez Airport, main hall, tel. 01/574-8000, www.peru.travel, 24 hours daily). There are other branches in San Isidro (Jorge Basadre 610, tel. 01/421-1627, 9am-6pm Mon.-Fri.) and Miraflores (Larcomar, tel. 01/445-9400, 11am-2pm and 3pm-8pm daily).

The best source of travel information in Peru, along with maps, advice, trip reports, restaurant and hotel discounts, and all-around friendly people, is the amazing Miraflores-based **South American Explorers Club** (Enrique Palacios 956, Miraflores, tel. 01/445-3306, www.saexplorers.org, 9:30am-5pm Mon.-Fri., 9:30am-1pm Sat.).

In Barranco, **Intej** (San Martín 240, tel. 01/247-3230, www.intej.org, 9am-1pm and 2pm-6:30pm Mon.-Fri., 9am-1pm Sat.) is the Lima base for all student travel organizations. Student travel cards can be acquired here with a letter on the appropriate school stationery, and student flights can be changed.

MAPS

The easiest place to buy maps is in Miraflores at the **South American Explorers Club** (Enrique Palacios 956, tel. 01/445-3306, www.saexplorers.org, 9:30am-5pm Mon.-Fri., 9:30am-1pm Sat.), which has good maps of Lima, the Huaraz area, and Peru in general. It also sells the more popular of Peru's military topographic maps.

For hard-to-find topo maps, head to Surquillo and the **Instituto Geográfico Nacional** (Aramburu 1190, tel. 01/475-9960, www.ign.gob.pe, 8:30am-4:45pm Mon.-Fri.), which also sells digital, geological, and departmental maps.

POLICE AND FIRE

Through **Iperú's** 24-hour stand (tel. 01/574-8000) in the main hall of the airport, you can report tourism-related crimes. The headquarters of the **national police** (Pezet y Miel 1894, www.pnp.gob.pe) are in Lince, and the **tourist police** (Moore 268, Magdalena, tel. 01/460-0849, dipolture@hotmail.com) have an office in Magdalena. Dialing 105 also reaches police from a private phone. You can also call neighborhood security, called Serenazgo. For central Lima dial 01/318-5050, for Miraflores dial 01/313-3773, for San Isidro dial 01/319-0450 and for Barranco call 01/719-2055. For the fire department, dial 116 or 421-2620.

IMMIGRATIONS OFFICE

Lima's **Migraciones** (immigration office, España 734, Breña, tel. 01/200-1000, 8am-1pm Mon.-Fri.) is near the center. Arrive early and with US$20 if you want to receive a new visa the same day.

HEALTH CARE

Lima has Peru's best hospitals, and it is easy, and quite inexpensive, to get parasite tests and yellow fever or tetanus shots.

Perhaps the easiest option, if you need a doctor, is to call **Doctor Más** (tel. 01/626-8888, ext. 0 for emergencies, ext. 1 to make an appointment), a company that, for US$45, will send an English-speaking doctor to your hotel to check on you and write a prescription. You can even pay with a credit card if you notify them while setting up the visit.

If you prefer a clinic, all of the places listed here have English-speaking doctors. In central Lima, the **Clínica International** (Washington 1471, 7:30am-9pm Mon.-Fri., 7:30am-5pm Sat.) will see walk-in patients for about US$30. Doctor's visits cost around US$30.

The best (and most expensive) medical care in Peru is in San Isidro at the **Clínica Anglo-Americana** (Alfredo Salazar, block 3 s/n, tel. 01/616-8900, www.angloamericana.com.pe, 9am-9pm daily), which charges US$90 for a doctor's visit.

In Miraflores, a high-quality option is **Clínica**

Good Hope (Malecón Balta 956, tel. 01/610-7300, www.goodhope.org.pe, 9am-midnight daily), which charges about US$60 for a doctor's visit. For lab testing and shots, **Suiza Lab** (Angamos Oeste 300, tel. 01/612-6666, www.suizalab.com,7am-6pm Sat., 7am-1pm Sun.) is very professional, clean, and reasonably priced. For dental problems, try the English-speaking Dr. Flavio Vásquez (Paseo de la República 6010, Suite 903, Miraflores, tel. 01/445-2586 or 9978-87977, emergencies 24 hours daily).

Pharmacies

Pharmacies are common in Lima, and most of them are willing to deliver to your hotel. Near central Lima, the **Metro supermarket** (Venezuela and Alfonso Ugarte) in Breña has a good pharmacy. In San Isidro, try **InkaFarma** (Camino Real 1301, tel. 01/314-2020, www.inkafarma.com.pe), which also has several locations in Miraflores. Other options in Miraflores include **Farmacias 24 Horas** (corner of Pardo and Comandante Espinar, Miraflores, tel. 01/444-0568, 24 hours daily), and **Botica Fasa** (Larco 747, tel. 01/619-0000, www.boticasfasa.com.pe, 24-hour delivery).

BANKS AND MONEY EXCHANGE

For those just arriving in Peru, there are two exchange houses inside the Lima airport that change traveler's checks for a 2.5 percent commission. In general, the best place to cash traveler's checks is at any Banco de Crédito, which charges the lowest commission—1.8 percent. ATMs are now ubiquitous across Lima and most of Peru. Almost all work with Visa, MasterCard, and Cirrus, and Interbank's Global Net and Banco de Crédito even handle American Express. Take care when getting money at night; it's a good idea to have a taxi waiting and to go with a friend.

Money-exchange businesses (*casas de cambio*) offer slightly better rates than banks and are mercifully free of the hour-long lines that snake inside most banks. There are a few exchange businesses on Larco in Miraflores and on Ocoña in central Lima. Be careful changing

money with people on the street, even if they do have the requisite badge and bright-colored vest. Safe places for changing money on the street are Parque Kennedy or Pardo and Comandante Espinar in Miraflores.

Here is an alphabetical listing of banks and money changers by neighborhood. Banks are generally open 9am-6pm Monday-Friday and 9am-12:30pm Saturday. All banks are closed on Sunday.

In central Lima, there's **Banco Continental** (Abancay 260-262, tel. 01/595-0000), **Banco de Crédito** (Venezuela 1202, tel. 01/311-9898), **Interbank** (Jr. de la Unión 600), **Scotiabank** (Camaná 623-627, tel. 01/211-6000).

San Isidro, Lima's financial district, has a **Banco Continental** (Camino Real 355 second floor), **Banco de Crédito** (Jorge Basadre 301), an **Interbank** (Jorge Basadre 391-395), **Scotiabank** (Carnaval y Moreyra 282), and **Western Union** (Petit Thouars 3595, tel. 01/422-0014).

Miraflores's banks are generally clustered around the Parque Kennedy: **American Express** (Santa Cruz 621, Miraflores, tel. 01/710-3900, 9am-5:30pm Mon.-Fri., 9am-1pm Sat.), which will replace its traveler's checks; **Banco Continental** (Pardo 791-795); **Banco de Crédito** (Av. Larco 611); **Interbank** (Larco 690); **Scotiabank** (Av. Diagonal 176); and a **Western Union** (Larco 826, tel. 01/459-5368).

Barranco's selection of financial institutions are **Banco Continental** (Grau 414), **Banco de Crédito** (José M. Eguren 599, Ex-Grau), **Interbank** (Grau 300), and **Scotiabank** (Grau 422).

COMMUNICATIONS

Peru's national postal service (www.serpost.com.pe) has several offices in Lima; and you can find a **post office** (Camana 790, tel. 01/426-1780, 8am-7pm Mon.-Fri., 8am-4pm Sat.) in central Lima. The **Miraflores post office** (Petit Thouars 5201, tel. 01/445-0697, 8am-9pm Mon.-Sat., 9am-2pm Sun.) has slightly different hours. There are also courier services from **FedEx** (Pasaje Olaya 260,

newspaper stand

Miraflores, tel. 01/242-2280) and **DHL** (2 de Mayo 595, San Isidro, tel. 01/221-0816).

High-speed Internet access is ubiquitous in Lima. In central Lima, try **Internet** (Pasaje Santa Rosa 165, Center, 7:30am-2pm daily, US$0.75 per hour). Recommended places in Miraflores are **Alf.net** (Manuel Bonilla 126), **Refugio Internet** (Larco 1185), and the helpful and cheap **Via Planet** (Diez Canseco 339). These places do Internet calls as well.

For national calls, buy a 147 card and dial away from Telefónica booths on nearly every corner. For international calls, put away those phone cards, because new-generation cable and satellite shops offer crystal-clear communication for as low as US$0.15 per minute to the United States. **Call Center USA** (Junín 410, 4 blocks toward Vía Expresa from Av. Arequipa) offers cable calls to the United States, Europe, or Asia. This place also has high-speed Internet.

NEWSPAPERS

Lima's largest newspapers are **El Comercio** (www.elcomercioperu.pe) and **La República**
(www.larepublica.com.pe), the latter which publishes a column by Mario Vargas Llosa. A popular weekly magazine for news, humor and cultural information is **Caretas. Poder** has articles by one of Peru's best investigative journalists, Ricardo Uceda. **Etiqueta Negra** (www.etiquetanegra.com.pe) is a literary and social commentary magazine, and **Bocón** (www.elbocon.com.pe) is the soccer paper. The best free sources of English-language news are **Peruvian Times** (www.peruvian-times.com) and **Peru This Week** (www.pe-ruthisweek.com).

LANGUAGE SCHOOLS

There are many Spanish schools in Lima, although getting away from all the English speakers is a challenge. A favorite school is **El Sol** (Grimaldo de Solar 469, Miraflores, tel. 01/242-7763, www.idiomasperu.com), which has several programs for travelers at the basic level and for those that are more fluent. The school offers students cooking and dancing classes, city walks, volunteer opportunities, conversation workshops, and family homestays. A week of El Sol's intensive program (20 hours per week) is US$293, while it also offers a semi-intensive (10 hours per week) for US$156. You can brush up on your Spanish before your trip and keep up with your studies afterward with El Sol's **Web Spanish** (www. webspanish.com), which provides one-on-one Spanish classes online.

Also in Miraflores is **Hispana** (San Martín 377, tel. 01/446-3045, www.hispanaidiomas. com), which offers classes one-on-one and in small groups. A 20-hour week of the intensive study program in a small group runs US$240. It offers homestays with a Peruvian family and also has a student residence.

In San Isidro, language schools include the **Instituto de Idiomas** (Camino Real 1037, tel. 01/626-6500, www.idiomas.pucp.edu.pe), which charges US$130 for 36 hours of lessons. The institute is part of Peru's top university, the **Pontificia Universidad Católica del Perú.** You can also hire a private tutor. For one-on-one lessons, some recommended private tutors are **Lourdes Galvez** (tel. 01/435-3910, US$8 per hour) and **Alex Boris** (tel. 01/423-0697, US$8 per hour).

FILM AND CAMERAS

Lima's best film-developing and camera-repair shop is **Taller de Fotografía Profesional** (Benavides 1171, tel. 01/628-5915, 9am-7pm Mon.-Fri., 9:30am-1pm Sun.). Other top-quality developing with one-day service is available from **Laboratorio Color Profesional** (Benavides 1171, tel. 01/214-8430, 9am-7pm Mon.-Fri., 9:30am-1pm Sat.). A cheaper option is **Kodak Express** (Larco 1005, Miraflores, tel. 01/241-6515; Las Begonias 1370, San Isidro, tel. 01/441-2800; Grau 675, Barranco; 9am-9pm Mon.-Sat.). For digital camera technical glitches, contact **Jorge Li Pun** (General Silva 496, Miraflores, tel. 01/447-7302, 10:30am-8pm Mon.-Fri.).

LAUNDRY

In Breña try **Lavandería KIO** (España 481, tel. 01/332-9035, 9am-8pm Mon.-Sat.). In San Isidro, **Lava Center** (Víctor Maurtua 140, tel. 01/440-3600, 10am-6pm Mon.-Sat.) is reliable. Recommended places in Miraflores are **Servirap** (Schell 601, Miraflores, tel. 01/241-0759, 8am-9pm Mon.-Sat., 10am-6pm Sun.), which offers drop-off and self-service, and **Lavandería Cool Wash** (Diez Canseco 347, Miraflores, tel. 01/242-3882, 8:30am-7:30pm Mon.-Sat.).

LUGGAGE STORAGE

Besides your hotel, you can also store bags at the airport for US$8 per day. **South American Explorers Club** members can store luggage at the clubhouse (Enrique Palacios 956, Miraflores) free of charge.

Getting There and Around

AIR

Lima's international airport is **Jorge Chávez** (tel. 01/511-6055, www.lap.com.pe), 16 kilometers west of the city center at Callao.

The leading domestic airline, with international flights as well, is **LAN** (Pardo 513, Miraflores, tel. 01/213-8200, www.lan.com). It flies to all major Peruvian airports, including Trujillo, Chiclayo, Tumbes, Arequipa, Cusco, Puerto Maldonado, and Juliaca. LAN charges non-Peruvian residents a separate, much more expensive fare for domestic flights than it does local residents. If you are not a Peruvian resident and you purchase the cheaper fare online, you will likely be charged the extra when you check in at the airport.

Other airlines for domestic flights are **StarPerú** (Pardo 485, Miraflores, tel. 01/242-7720, www.starperu.com.pe) and **Taca** (Pardo 811, Miraflores, www.taca.com), which also has international flights. There are also **Peruvian Airlines** (Pardo 495, Miraflores, tel.

01/715-6122, www.peruvian.pe), with flights to Cusco, Iquitos and Arequipa, and **LC Perú** (Pablo Carriquirry 857, San Isidro, tel. 01/204-1313, www.lcperu.com), with flights to smaller cities like Cajamarca, Huaraz, and Ayacucho.

All of the international airlines that fly into Peru also have offices in Lima, including **Aerolíneas Argentinas** (Dean Valdivia 243, Of. 301, San Isidro, tel. 01/513-6565, www.aerolineas.com.ar), **Aeroméxico** (Pardo y Aliaga 699, Of. 501-C, San Isidro, tel. 01/705-1111, www.aeromexico.com), **Air Canada** (Italia 389, Of. 101, Miraflores, tel. 0800-52073, www.aircanada.com), **American Airlines** (Basadre 265, San Isidro, tel. 01/211-7000, www.aa.com.pe), **United Airlines** (Víctor Andrés Belaúnde 147, Of. 101, San Isidro, tel. 01/712-9230, www.united.com), **Copa Airlines** (Los Halcones 105, San Isidro, tel. 01/610-0808, www.copaair.com), and **Delta Air Lines** (Víctor Andrés Belaúnde 147, Torre Real 3, San Isidro, tel. 01/211-9211, www.delta.com).

BUS

Highways in Peru have improved immensely over the last decade, making in-country bus travel not only cheap but efficient. Still, if you have the option, don't take night buses, as they are more prone to accidents, especially when traveling in the Andes. From Lima, buses head to every major city in Peru except water-locked Iquitos. The **South American Explorers Club** (Enrique Palacios 956, Miraflores, tel. 01/445-3306, www.saexplorers.org, 9:30am-5pm Mon.-Fri., 9:30am-1pm Sat.) has an excellent Lima folder with a detailed rundown of bus companies and their schedules. Unfortunately, there is no main bus station in Lima. Instead, companies have their own terminals in the center and sometimes also on Javier Prado or Paseo de la República near San Isidro. If you can, take a bus from one of the terminals on Javier Prado. The area is closer to Miraflores, San Isidro, and Barranco, and safer than some of the neighborhoods around the central terminals. Take a taxi to and from the terminal and keep a hand on all your belongings.

The two classic and reputable bus companies in Lima are Cruz del Sur and Ormeño. Móvil Tours and Oltursa, however, both get consistently strong reviews. **Cruz del Sur** (tel. 01/311-5050, www.cruzdelsur.com.pe) has a terminal in the center (Quilca 531) and near San Isidro (Javier Prado Este 1100). Although it does not go as many places as Ormeño, Cruz del Sur's Cruzero is the most comprehensive bus service in Peru. Best of all, tickets can be bought instantly online, from any agency in Lima, or at the TeleTicket counters at Wong and Metro supermarkets (in Miraflores there is a Wong at Óvalo Gutierrez and a Metro at Schell 250, near Parque Kennedy). Spanish speakers can even call the Cruz del Sur call center (tel. 01/311-5050, have your passport number ready) and have their tickets delivered free of charge. Payment is in cash upon receipt of tickets. Buses leave first from the central Lima terminal and pick up passengers a half hour later at the Javier Prado terminal. For complete route information, see the company's website.

Ormeño (tel. 01/427-5679, www.grupo-ormeno.com) also has a terminal in the center (Carlos Zavala 177) and an international terminal near San Isidro (Javier Prado Este 1059, La Victoria, tel. 01/472-1710). Ormeño has better coverage and is slightly cheaper than Cruz del Sur. To buy an Ormeño ticket, visit a terminal, go through an agency (the agency will get the tickets a few hours later), or call the Spanish-only call center (tel. 01/472-5000). Again, have your passport number when calling and cash in hand when the ticket is delivered.

The highly recommended **Móvil Tours** (Paseo de la República 749, La Victoria, tel. 01/523-2385, www.moviltours.com.pe) has a station near San Isidro and runs mainly to the northern cities, including Huaraz, Chachapoyas, and Chiclayo, and fares are about the same as Ormeño.

The local favorite, **Oltursa** (Av. Aramburu 1160, Surquillo, tel. 01/708-5000, www.oltursa.pe), runs primarily a coastal route both north and south of Lima, along with routes to Arequipa and Chiclayo. The company comes highly recommended for its service (some claim that it's better than Cruz del Sur), and advance reservations can be made by telephone or on-line. You can buy your ticket by phone or at the **Tu Entrada** stands in Plaza Vea or Vivanda grocery stores. Tickets can also be delivered.

Phone reservations do not work well at the other companies; the best bet is to buy tickets at the terminal.

Expreso Wari (Luna Pizarro 34, La Victoria, tel. 01/330-3518) goes to Nasca, Ayacucho, and Cusco. **Flores** (tel. 01/332-1212, www.floresh-nos.net) has the best coverage of the small bus companies, lower fares, and a terminal in both central Lima (Montevideo 523) and near San Isidro (Paseo de la República 627, La Victoria). It has cheap buses for Arequipa, Cajamarca, Chiclayo, Nasca, Piura, Puno, Tacna, Trujillo, and Tumbes. **Soyuz** (México 280, tel. 01/205-2370, www.soyuz.com.pe) has good frequency on the south coast.

Companies whose travelers report frequent delays, breakdowns, or other problems include **Tepsa** and **Civa.** Recommended international companies are Ormeño and **Caracol** (Plaza Norte Local 120, corner of Tupac Amaru and Tomás Valle, Independencia, tel. 01/431-1400, www.perucaracol.com), which receives the best reviews and covers the entire continent. It partners with Cruz del Sur so you can buy tickets from either company's terminals. Among other places, Caracol travels to Santiago, Chile; Santa Cruz and La Paz, Bolivia; Asunción, Paraguay; Córdoba and Buenos Aires, Argentina; Montevideo, Uruguay; São Paulo and Rio de Janeiro, Brazil; and Quito and Guayaquil, Ecuador.

Ormeño (Javier Prado Este 1059, tel. 01/472-1710) no longer travels to Brazil but runs buses to Bogotá, Colombia; Santiago, Chile; Buenos Aires, Argentina; and Guayaquil, Ecuador.

TRAIN

Between late March and early November, a passenger train still departs on Friday from Lima's antique Desamparados train station downtown. After climbing the steep valley above Lima it crests the Andes at a breathtaking 4,751 meters and continues to Huancayo. Trains return from Huancayo to Lima on Sunday evening, making for an interesting weekend outing. Tickets can be bought at the offices of **Ferrocarril Central Andino** (José Galvez Barrenchea 566, 5th Fl., San Isidro, tel. 01/226-6363, www.ferrocar-rilcentral.com.pe) or from **Tu Entrada** (tel. 01/618-3838, www.tuentrada.com.pe).

LOCAL TRANSPORTATION

Taxi

If you want to make a spare buck in Lima, buy a taxi sticker from the market for US$0.50, plop it on your windshield, and start picking up passengers. Understandably, the vast majority of taxis in Lima are unofficial and unregulated, and assaults on passengers picked up at the airport occur occasionally.

The best way to take a taxi is to call a registered company and pay an additional 30-50 percent. Recommended taxi companies include **Taxi Lima** (tel. 01/213-5050, daily 24 hours), **Taxi Miraflores** (tel. 01/477-1743, daily 24 hours), and **Taxi Móvil** (tel. 01/422-6890, San Isidro, daily 24 hours). To and from the airport, **Taxi Green** (tel. 01/484-4001) is recommended.

If you feel comfortable, and have a smidgen of Spanish, stand on the street until a safe-looking registered taxi passes by. These should be painted yellow and have the taxi sign on the hood of the car and a registration sticker on the windshield. Older taxi drivers tend to be safer than young ones. Of course, avoid old cars with tinted windows and broken door handles. Bargain before you get in a taxi or you will get fleeced. Fares from the airport to Miraflores should be US$15-20, from the airport to the center about US$15, from Miraflores to the center about US$6, and Miraflores to Barranco about US$4. Prices go up during rush hour and at night. Taxis can also be rented by the hour for US$12 (registered taxi) or US$8 (street taxi).

Bus

In 2010, Lima got its first rapid transit system, called **El Metropolitano** (www.metro-politano.com.pe). Metropolitano buses run a 30-kilometer line from the seaside neighborhood of Chorrillos through Barranco

Lima Bus Schedule

The following is a thumbnail of bus trip duration and prices to and from Lima with a range from economical to luxury service. At the bottom end, buses stop frequently, are crowded, and lack restrooms. The top-end buses are decked out with reclining semi-beds, clean restrooms, onboard food and beverage service, video, and a second story with great views. Prices increase 50 percent around holidays, including Christmas, Easter, and the July 28 Fiestas Patrias weekend.

City	Price	Time
Arequipa	US$20-50	13-15 hours
Ayacucho	US$20-35	9-10 hours
Cajamarca	US$25-48	14 hours
Chachapoyas	US$20-50	22 hours
Chanchamayo	US$10-27	8 hours
Chiclayo	US$19-40	12 hours
Cusco	US$30-50	21 hours
Huancayo	US$17-30	7 hours
Huaraz	US$15-26	8 hours
Máncora	US$28-60	16-17 hours
Nasca	US$15-40	8 hours
Pisco	US$13-28	4 hours
Piura	US$25-50	15-16 hours
Puno	US$34-60	21-24 hours
Tacna	US$37-60	18-20 hours (Chile border)
Trujillo	US$20-42	8 hours
Tumbes	US$30-60	18 hours (Ecuador border)

Miraflores and San Isidro to central Lima and beyond. This is the best public transportation to and from central Lima: It's faster, safer, and better on the environment. Fares are about US$0.75 and are paid using a reusable prepaid electronic card that can be bought at any station. There are five stations in Miraflores (28 de Julio, Benavides, Ricardo Palma, Angamos, and Domingo Orué), three in San Isidro (Aramburú, Canaval y Moreyra, and Javier Prado), and four in Barranco (Estadio Unión, Bulevar, Balta, and Plaza de Flores). There are several stations in the center, including the Estadio Nacional, located on the outskirts of downtown just outside the soccer stadium and close to Parque de la Exposición, as well as the Estación Central Grau and Jirón de la Unión. There is an express lane and another lane where the buses stop at each station. Visit the website for a map of the route and stations.

Traveling to other parts of Lima are the notorious *combi*, or minivan-type buses, and other, larger buses. These beat-up vehicles race through Lima's main streets crammed full of passengers and blaring anything from 1980s pop songs to *cumbia* or salsa. Managing these buses is a two-person job: one person is behind the wheel and the other has their head out the window yelling to onlookers where the bus is going and collecting fares from passengers. You can also tell the buses route by the sticker on the front windshield. Fares start at about US$0.30 and increase depending on the distance. To get off simply say *"baja"* ("getting off") or *"esquina"* ("at the corner").

Car Rental

The major rental car agencies are **Hertz** (Diez Canseco 218, Miraflores, tel. 01/445-5716, www.hertz.com.pe), **Budget** (Larco 998, Miraflores, tel. 01/444-4546, airport tel. 01/517-1880, www.budgetperu.com), and **Avis** (28 de Julio 587, Miraflores, tel. 01/444-0450, airport tel. 01/517-1847, www.avisperu.com).

Private Car

Private drivers can also be hired for the hour, day, or for a trip like the Nasca Lines. Many travelers who are only in Lima for a single day would greatly benefit from a driver who recommends museums and restaurants and then drops them off at the airport in the evening. A highly recommended driver is **José Salinas Casanova** (tel. 932-92614, casanovacab@hotmail.com, US$10 per hour), based at the Hotel Antigua Miraflores. **Marcelino Cardena** (tel. 989-840284, US$10 per hour) is also based at the Antigua Miraflores. You can also try English-speaking **Mónica Velasquez** (tel. 994-30796 or 01/224-8608).

Southern Beaches

During Lima's summer months the beaches just south of the city are a popular weekend destination for students, office workers, families, and world-class surfers. Though they can be crowded, this is a good place to go if you need a beach fix, and it's much closer than taking a 20-hour bus trip to Peru's northern beaches.

Popular beach towns just south of Lima are Punta Hermosa and San Bartolo. You will find sandy beaches, world-class surfing waves, protected beaches for safe swimming, rocking nightlife, a few good hostels, and lots of *cebicherías*. The only time to visit these beaches is during the summer months, from mid-December to the end of April—skies are cloudy during the rest of the year. Make reservations well in advance, especially January to mid-March, when surfers from around the world flock here along with Peruvian students on summer break. The best time to go is Sunday-Thursday nights, when beaches are empty and hotel prices are often 30 percent lower than the weekend rates.

There are other options besides Punta Hermosa and San Bartolo. **Santa María,** at Km 48 of the Panamericana, is an upscale beach with a control point that admits only residents and respectable-looking day-trippers, though there are few or no lodging options. **Pucusana** is a picturesque fishing town at Km 58 of the Panamericana. **Puerto Viejo,** at Km 72 of the Panamericana, is a long beach good for beginning surfers—including a left point break that ranges 1-2 meters. **Leon Dormido** (Sleeping Lion) at Km 80 has a calm beach that is often crowded. The best parties are at **Asia,** at Km 97, which becomes an explosion of discos, condos, private clubs, and even car dealerships in the summer. Teenagers here for the parties pack the beach and the discos at night. Near Asia's beaches, and close to shore, there are several islands with great sea kayaking and possibilities to see Humboldt penguins and sea lions. Finally, **Cerro Azul,** at Km 128, is a forgotten port, with a small fishing community and a pleasant beach with both pipeline and beginner waves for all levels of surfers.

PUNTA HERMOSA

Thirty minutes south of Lima at Km 40 on the Panamericana, Punta Hermosa is a bigtime surfing destination with a great range of beaches and services. It is here that **Pico Alto,** the largest wave in South America, forms in May and reaches heights up to 12 meters. The town itself is on a rocky peninsula, called La Isla, which is surrounded by seven beaches. From north to south, these are El Silencio, Caballeros, Señoritas, Pico Alto, Playa Norte, La Isla, and Kontiki. When covered in rocks and not sand June-November, Playa Norte is a good place to get away from the crowds, along with Kontiki. But wherever you stay in Punta

Hermosa, these beaches are no more than 30 minutes' walk away.

Entertainment and Events

Every May or June, during the first big swell of the year, Punta Hermosa comes alive with Peru's annual big-wave competition. There is no fixed date for the competition, and it is usually organized within a week or two—check out **Buoyweather** (www.buoyweather.com, a paid site) or **Stormsurf** (www.stormsurf.com, free) for the right ocean conditions, or check **Perú azul** (www.peruazul.com), the country's premier surfing website.

Recreation

Punta Hermosa has several places to rent a board and a wetsuit, get an instructor, and **surf** a variety of waves from gentle to suicidal. The best beginner beaches in Punta Hermosa are Caballeros, Pacharacas, and La Isla. Taxis and surfing camps can arrange transportation to beginner beaches farther south, such as Puerto Viejo and Cerro Azul.

The honest and straightforward **Marco León Villarán** (tel. 01/230-8351, www.peruadventure.com), who runs a bed-and-breakfast in town, can arrange a variety of fabulous adventures in the area. His main passion is **spearfishing,** and if you have the snorkel, fins, and mask he can lead you to just about any fish you have ever dreamed of seeing—or spearing—including 1.2-meter yellowtail or gigantic flounder near Punta Hermosa.

Marco is also a professional bone-and-fossil hunter who knows Peru's desert coastline very well—from the fossil-rich deserts of Ica to the pristine and remote surfing beaches north of Chiclayo. He owns a reliable 4WD van and is an excellent, affordable, and trustworthy option for getting into remote areas of the Ica desert.

Accommodations and Food

Punta Hermosa's better places are in La Planicie, a quiet neighborhood to the north of town that offers a nice respite from the rowdy surfer scene in town, a 10-minute walk away.

A good restaurant and Internet access are here, along with Señoritas and Caballeros beaches. There are more hotels and nightlife, and the monster Pico Alto wave itself, near the center of Punta Hermosa—along with crowds of rowdy Brazilian and Argentinean surfers who are in town to test their mettle on waves that have made Punta Hermosa known as the Hawaii of South America.

In the Planicie neighborhood, longtime Punta Hermosa resident Marco León Villarán offers something for everyone at the **Peru Adventure Lodge** (Block Ñ, Lote 1, La Planicie, tel. 01/230-8351, www.peruadventure.com, US$20 pp). His rooms are quiet, large, and comfortable, with tons of hot water and two Labrador retrievers who can lick you awake every morning for a bit extra. He and his wife, Gloria, prepare excellent meals. The family rents out boards and also organizes surf and fossil tours all along the Peruvian coast.

In Punta Hermosa, another camp is run by Oscar Morante, a surf guide who leads trips all around Peru for several international surfing agencies. His **Pico Alto International Surf Camp** (Block L, Lote 14, tel. 01/230-7297, www.picoalto.com.pe) is well worth it.

There are many seafood restaurants, but probably the safest is **La Rotonda** (Bolognesi 592, tel. 01/230-7266, 8am-11pm daily, US$8). Apart from ceviche, the restaurant also does *chicharrón* and grilled fish, serving on a second-story deck with good views of surfers on Pico Alto. Another option is **Cebichería Carmencita** (Malecón de Punta Hermosa 821, tel. 01/9976-4792, 7am-10pm daily, US$5), which serves a range of fish dishes.

Getting There and Around

Probably the easiest way to get to Punta Hermosa from Lima is to hire a taxi (US$18) or arrange a pickup through your hotel. **Flavio Solaria** (tel. 01/230-7578, srtsurfcamp@yahoo.com) picks up groups from the Lima airport for US$30. Buses from Lima for Mala—which stop outside of Punta Hermosa, San Bartolo, and Santa María—pick up passengers at the circle, or *trébol,* where Avenida Javier Prado intersects with the Panamericana in Monterrico. These buses, called Maleños, take 45 minutes to reach Punta Hermosa and charge US$1.50.

Three-wheeled *motocars* abound in Punta Hermosa and are an option for getting between La Planicie and the town center (US$0.50).

SAN BARTOLO

Farther down the Panamericana, past an exclusive area of homes perched on a seaside cliff and an exclusive beach club known as La Quebrada, lies the laid-back beach town of San Bartolo. The town itself is perched on a bluff above an attractive horseshoe-shaped beach, lined with hotels, condos, and a *malecón,* known as Playa Norte. San Bartolo is less of a surfer party spot than the center of Punta Hermosa, with Peñascal, a right reef break that gets as high as four meters on the south end of the Playa Norte. There are gentler waves and a good place for swimming on the north end of Playa Norte, along with a few nice beachfront hotels. After entering from Km 48 of the Panamericana, the main drag into town is Avenida San Bartolo.

Accommodations and Food

Prices in San Bartolo double on weekend nights, so if you are planning a budget trip, make sure to visit during weekdays. Prices listed are for weekdays.

Great service and plush surroundings can be found at **Sol y Mar** (Malecón 930, tel. 01/430-7096, www.solymarperu.com US$30 s, US$48 d), with white leather couches, huge tiled rooms, great baths, cable TV, fridges, full kitchens in a few rooms, and terraces with great ocean-view rooms. The other nice place on Playa Norte is **La Posada del Mirador** (Malecón 105, tel. 01/430-7822, US$30 s, US$40 d, with breakfast), with furnished apartments.

Hostal 110 (San Martín Norte 110, tel. 01/430-7559, www.hostal110.com, US$60) has six small but clean rooms, each with a mini fridge and a TV, overlooking the bay. The hotel, which has two swimming pools, also has two-bedroom apartments (US$230 per week) that it rents by the week. For small groups, this is a much better and cheaper option.

Most of the eating options—except for the spit-roasted chicken at Mar Pacífico 495—revolve around seafood. There's a line of restaurants down Mar Pacífico. The best of these include **El Arador del Mar** (Mar Pacífico, tel. 01/430-8215, US$3-5), with a good seafood lunch menu for US$5. But the **El Rincón de Chelulo** (Mar Pacífico s/n, tel. 01/430-7170) wins out for a greater variety of fish and shellfish, unbelievable friendly service, and a larger US$3 lunch menu. These restaurants are in front of the plaza where the town's market opens up every morning. This square also has a few ice cream shops and pizzerias open in summer only.

Getting There and Around

Probably the easiest way to get to San Bartolo from Lima is to hire a taxi (US$20) or take the Cruz del Sur bus, which stops at the town entrance. Local buses from Lima for Mala—which stop outside of Punta Hermosa, San Bartolo, and Santa María—pick up passengers at the circle, or *trébol,* where Avenida Javier Prado intersects with the Panamericana in Barranco. These buses take 50 minutes to reach San Bartolo and charge US$1.50.

MAP SYMBOLS

═══	Expressway	**(**	Highlight	✈	Airport	⚲	Golf Course
───	Primary Road	○	City/Town	✗	Airfield	**P**	Parking Area
───	Secondary Road	◉	State Capital	▲	Mountain	▲	Archaeological Site
┈┈┈	Unpaved Road	✷	National Capital	✛	Unique Natural Feature	▮	Church
┈┈┈	Trail	★	Point of Interest			💂	Gas Station
┈┈┈	Ferry	●	Accommodation	╲	Waterfall	🐠	Dive Site
┄┄┄	Railroad	▼	Restaurant/Bar	⬥	Park		Mangrove
	Pedestrian Walkway	■	Other Location	**T**	Trailhead		Reef
ꭍꭍꭍꭍ	Stairs	Λ	Campground	☀	Lighthouse		Swamp

CONVERSION TABLES

°C = (°F - 32) / 1.8
°F = (°C x 1.8) + 32
1 inch = 2.54 centimeters (cm)
1 foot = 0.304 meters (m)
1 yard = 0.914 meters
1 mile = 1.6093 kilometers (km)
1 km = 0.6214 miles
1 fathom = 1.8288 m
1 chain = 20.1168 m
1 furlong = 201.168 m
1 acre = 0.4047 hectares
1 sq km = 100 hectares
1 sq mile = 2.59 square km
1 ounce = 28.35 grams
1 pound = 0.4536 kilograms
1 short ton = 0.90718 metric ton
1 short ton = 2,000 pounds
1 long ton = 1.016 metric tons
1 long ton = 2,240 pounds
1 metric ton = 1,000 kilograms
1 quart = 0.94635 liters
1 US gallon = 3.7854 liters
1 Imperial gallon = 4.5459 liters
1 nautical mile = 1.852 km

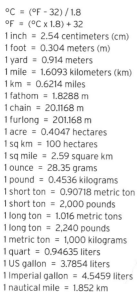

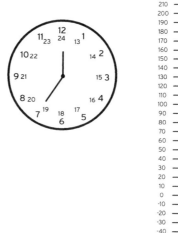

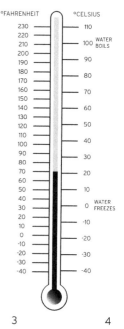

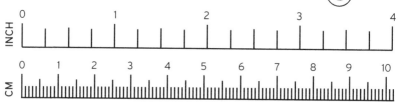

MOON SPOTLIGHT LIMA

Avalon Travel
a member of the Perseus Books Group
1700 Fourth Street
Berkeley, CA 94710, USA
www.moon.com

Editor: Erin Raber
Series Manager: Kathryn Ettinger
Copy Editor: Christopher Church
Graphics and Production Coordinator: Lucie Ericksen
Cover Design: Faceout Studios, Charles Brock
Moon Logo: Tim McGrath
Map Editor: Mike Morgenfeld
Cartographer: Paige Enoch

ISBN-13: 978-1-61238-781-9

Title page photo: Plaza Mayor, celebration of national
independence © Ksenia Ragozina/123RF

Printed in the United States of America

ABOUT THE AUTHORS

Ryan Dubé

Ryan Dubé first arrived in Peru more than a decade ago, as an exchange student in Lima. He was captivated by the country's diversity and history and charmed by the kindness of its people. After completing his degree in Latin American studies and anthropology, Ryan returned to Lima where he now lives with his wife, Tatiana, and their son, Ticiano.

Using Lima as his base, Ryan has traveled throughout Peru. He has hiked the Inca Trail to Machu Picchu, explored the islands on Lake Titicaca, and slept under the stars in the Amazon. He has traveled to Chincha and El Carmen, the home of an annual Afro-Peruvian music festival, and Pozuzo, a remote village in the high jungle.

Ryan currently works as a journalist, specializing in economics, business, and politics. His articles have been published in The Wall Street Journal, The Globe & Mail, and BNamericas, among others.

DATE DUE

3 4015 07141 1639

CPSIA information can be obtained at www.ICGtesting.com
Printed in the USA
LVOW01s1330220814

400058LV00005B/18/P

9 781612 387819